Canada Our Century

100 Voices · 500 Visions

Original text by Mark Kingwell and Christopher Moore

Photo research and visual narrative by Sara Borins

Doubleday Canada
an Otherwise Inc. Edition

Canada: Our Century was produced by Otherwise Inc. Editions
under the direction of Sara Borins
Graphic design by Concrete Design Communications Inc.
Captions and editorial direction by Rick Archbold
Editorial assistance by Jennifer Heyns

Otherwise Inc. Editions offers special thanks to Michael Angel,
Rick Archbold, Anne-Marie Beaton, Gus and Maria Bohlig, Adeline Borins,
Edward and Eva Borins, David and Daniel Borins, Stephen Bulger,
the Canadian Museum of Contemporary Photography, Serge Clement,
Dean Cooke, Barbara Czarnecki, Kelly Duffin, Bryce Duffy, Greig Dymond,
Rick Feldman, Mark Friesen, Andrea Gordon, Jennifer Heyns, Sam Hiyate,
Christine Innes, Martha Kanya-Forstner, Diti Katona, Belinda Kemp,
Laurie and Anne Kingsland, Mark Kingwell, Sue Lagasi, Janine Laporte,
Jerry Levitan, Constance MacKenzie, Brad Martin, Maya Mavjee,
Alissa Mesner, Christopher Moore, Pat Morrow, the National Archives
of Canada, Charles Pachter, John Pearce, Belinda Peres, Andrew Podnieks,
Ron Poling, John Pylypczak, Lou Ann Sartori, Bree Seely, Maia-Marie
Sutnik, Gabor Szilasi, Henry Tyminski, Chris Wahl, Morris Wolfe

The imagined memoirs which open each decade in this book are fiction.
The speakers are not intended to resemble any actual persons living or dead.

Canadian Cataloguing in Publication Data

Kingwell, Mark Gerald
          Canada : our century : 100 voices, 500 visions

Includes index.
ISBN 0-385-25893-3

1. Canada — History — 20th century — Pictorial works.*
2. Canada — History — 20th century.
3. Canadian literature (English) — 20th century.*   I. Moore, Christopher.   II. Title.

FC600.K56 1999   971'.0022'2   C99-931390-8
F1026.K56 1999

Printed and bound in Canada

Produced by Otherwise Inc.   Published in Canada by Doubleday Canada,
356A Queen Street West   a division of Random House of Canada Ltd.
Toronto, Ontario   105 Bond Street
M5V 2A2   Toronto, Ontario
                                         M5B 1Y3

FRI   10   9   8   7   6   5   4   3   2   1

Contents

Canada in Focus Six Notes on How Worlds Are Made

1. Identities What makes a century? What makes a country?

This book, a history told with visions and voices, is an attempt to open up a space for reflection on what this century has been for Canadians. It records our efforts in diplomacy, art, sport, thinking, industry, and a thousand other human undertakings.

The 20th century has been many things, and even a partial list of superlatives would run to many pages: the fastest 100 years of human history, also the bloodiest, the most populous, the most rapacious, the most prosperous. Many of the things we now take for granted did not exist, or were not widely available, as the century opened: the household telephone, the automobile, airplanes, computers, the keyboard, highways, frozen food, instant coffee, painless dentistry, the satellite, compact discs, tanks, machine guns, and Prozac – to name just a few.

The century began with the world carved into empires. It ends likewise, though with the boundaries and categories of empire much altered. Corporations now wield more control than nations, individuals command more wealth than governments. The secular religion of capitalism has eliminated its competitors, for better and worse, and we now have a genuinely global world for perhaps the first time in history's memory. If the global culture we have is not, in its consumerism and technological dominance, the one we might have wished for – or the one envisioned by popular dreamers at the century's beginning – it nevertheless forces us to accept that we are all interdependent now.

Only about 30 million of the approximately 6 billion people on the planet today are Canadian: that is 0.5 percent, roughly one in 200. But Canadians have always, as they like to say in hockey, played bigger than they are. Whether the 20th century has really belonged to Canada, as Wilfrid Laurier famously predicted, is not a question this book attempts to answer; it is probably a question without an answer. Yet it is certainly true that Canada came into its own as a country in this 100-year span, moving from sparsely populated British dominion to independent power on the global stage.

The fabric of the nation changed decisively from agricultural to information-based – a story, as the political economist Harold Innis taught us to see, of communications technology in action, binding us together with steel and wire and electromagnetic signals across the vast expanse of our territory. Our population diversified and blossomed to such an extent that it is now possible to walk the streets of Vancouver or Toronto and not hear English spoken for many blocks.

Despite much hand-wringing, no dominant myths of our nationhood have emerged this century, no larger narratives of identity that give some other nations a way of looking at themselves. We have toyed with such myths and images, but the results have not been impressive. The federal government sold Disney our display rights to the Mountie icon. We talk about socialized medicine and our social safety net but love to complain about our tax burden and ailing dollar. We pride ourselves on a talent for diplomacy and "soft power" global influence yet surrender sovereignty to a visiting dictator who prefers not to be bothered by a few student protesters.

We have struggled to mould a version of liberal politics for this diverse nation, and to some extent we have succeeded. And yet the nation remains uneasy and provisional as the century closes, a loose and sometimes divisive collection of communities. A constitution was repatriated this century, by one of our history's most charismatic leaders, but Canada's constitutional crisis nevertheless continues, the constant background rhythm of our political symphony.

In short, all is not well as we cross into this new century, and new millennium, of the Common Era. But whatever ails us, it will not be solved by trying to tease out some simplistic story of our identity, some mass-market image of Canadianness. Any such story will be false, perhaps dangerously so. We should see this lack of common myths for the advantage it is, and finally accept with confidence the vividness and reality – if also the complexity and subtlety, the strength and weakness – of the Canadian character. We know who we are, even if we are not always able to say exactly what that is.

Canadians leave their mark on the century in countless ways. These pages capture some of them, and they include both the beauty and the heartbreak of the times. In many ways the book is a tribute, but we have not ignored the dark side of Canada's century, and we have not tried to lay out a specious "Great Nation" caricature, full of firsts and records and signs of making it good abroad. We have simply tried to give some sense of the range of life in this country over 100 years, to take a look at the faces and places that have made Canada what it is.

This history – any history – is necessarily limited, idiosyncratic, even a little peculiar now and then. We hope it is also stimulating, funny, moving, and beautiful. Like the country it depicts.

2. Moments Words run through the book, from the 100 neatly juxtaposed pieces of primary texts, to Christopher Moore's brilliantly reconstructed voices of each decade, to the captions on the photographs. But photographs, and the idea of the photograph, are at the centre of the book. Why do we choose this form of social record?

The simple answer – also the complex answer – is that photography is the technology of representation that most of us are closest to, the picture machine we all use as the century progresses. Who among us does not have a photo album of treasured memories stored somewhere? A wallet shot of a loved one? A pixel-scanned snap of a newborn child posted on a Web site? When television's recent dominance is placed in a larger historical context, we may even say that photography is the dominant visual medium of the century.

Consider the camera itself. Once the expensive toy of eccentric enthusiasts and trained professionals alone, it has been completely domesticated in this century, morphing from wild and unpredictable beast to taken-for-granted family pet. It becomes, in the process, a fixture of daily life. This did not happen quickly, the way the personal computer bullied its way onto our desktops in less than a decade; nor did it happen stealthily, the way the blue-glow box of television took up its dominating position in living-room corner and bedroom eyeline almost without our noticing it. It happened by stages that, like photographic images themselves, are distinct enough to see clearly. Or, to take a different metaphor from the same filmic stock, we can watch the picture come slowly into focus as the century proceeds.

That is a story of technology, but it is equally the story of a people as they struggle, like people everywhere, to make a record of their lives. Trapped in the relentless flow of time, we try to capture moments and document events. We attempt, as the Greek roots of "photograph" remind us, to write them in light. And we are conditioned, in ways we rarely realize, by the images that swim through and around us in the ether of our experience. Despite all that has happened in the fast-moving world of information technology, this is as true at century's end as when the era was born.

Thus it was possible for my grandfather, born in Quebec City in 1904, to remember photographs as the exclusive business of the portrait gallery, painterly in their pose and detail. Or to recall the first fuzzy photographic images that illustrated his daily newspaper. My father, born in the same city in 1933, was used to seeing photographs around him in the papers and magazines. He could even, as he entered adulthood, handle the technology himself. Little black-and-white snaps, some with those lovely old scalloped edges, record his romance with my mother, little tokens of affection she sent him, complete with sweetheart notes on the back in her looping, convent-school hand. A beautiful newspaper shot, flashbulbs all a-pop on his white tux and my mother's lacy dress, records their glamorous wedding a year later.

And I, born in Toronto in 1963, remember playing with a boxy old Brownie in my mother's mother's house on Van Dusen Boulevard, fiddling with its metal catches and off-centre shutter opening. The pictures stayed small, square three-by-threes that show my brother and me dressed in white shirts and dark ties, our hair slicked, ready to go to church. Or me in pedal-pushers and a baseball cap, looking into the southern Ontario sky as if it held the secrets of life. Our father props the two of us on his knees, smiling handsomely out of the frame, legs long in his pegged gabardine trousers, his hair piled Elvis-high.

I stand in the snow wearing an elaborate parka and shiny vinyl ski pants, looking confused, mittens dangling from my sleeves on woollen strings. Or I clutch a Bible, squinting into the camera through the sun, next to my brother. I am chubby and crew-cut, he is angular and bowl-trimmed. Our father is very tall. Sometimes he wears his smart flight lieutenant's uniform. Our mother is rarely seen – she is holding the camera, framing the world.

Later the photos pop into colour, the white borders and sharp edges replaced by satin finish, rounded corners, and tone bleeds right to the edge. My younger brother appears, also a dachshund called Mitzi. My father wears orange and brown, thinks better of it. He grows a moustache, thinks better of that. My mother's hair goes up high, comes down again. She wears Jackie O sunglasses and a snakeskin trenchcoat on a drive to Cavendish. She wears floor-length blue dresses, and yellow mini-skirts, and green pantsuits for fondue dinner parties and evenings at the officers' mess. She lifts a turkey out of a roasting pan.

My father plays his guitar, a stubby brown beer bottle near his feet. My brothers and I get taller and taller. Our hair gets longer and longer. We pose in Leafs jerseys and school jackets and First Communion albs. Our jeans bell at the bottom and then go straight. We are always opening presents in our tartan bathrobes. We play on the beach at Malpeque, shovel massive Winnipeg snowdrifts, wear ceremonial clothes in Lindsay, Toronto, Vancouver, New York, Edinburgh, and New Haven. We eat a lot of birthday cake.

Such are the moments that make a life.

3. Frames What is the essence of photography? Not so much the photosensitive film, really, as the dark box that contains it, the time-stealing camera that exposes the film in shutter-quick moments. Every photograph is framed in both time and space, an artificially preserved slice of reality rendered in the two relatively durable dimensions of paper. And, as with all slices, this one is remarkable as much for what it is *not* as for what it is.

"When a photograph is cropped," writes the philosopher Stanley Cavell, "the rest of the world is cut *out*. The implied presence of the rest of the world, and its explicit rejection, are as essential in the experience of a photograph as what it explicitly presents." The photograph frames what is, in experience, unframed: the space beyond the oblong picture, the time beyond the skewered moment.

Yet this framing, ostensibly a limitation on the presumed purpose of the camera – to snag some slab of reality, and stuff it into our hands – is precisely what makes the resulting image so powerful, so much worth a thousand words and more. "A camera is an opening in a box: that is the best emblem of the fact that a camera holding on an object is holding the rest of the world away," Cavell goes on. "The camera has been praised for extending the senses; it may, as the world goes, deserve more credit for confining them, leaving room for thought."

Seeing this, Cavell usefully reverses the standard McLuhanite wisdom that says technologies of communication are always extensions of the senses. He shows instead that real value sometimes lies in confining them. For here, with the world necessarily implied rather than experienced, we are forced, perhaps for the first time, to confront the fact of the world. The world held outside the frame is obtrusive because *not included*, and the photograph compels that awareness because it reminds us, in its very limitations, of what lies beyond limits.

As with space, so with time. The image is the crest of time briefly stopped, frozen in the frame. The future lies undetermined in these pictures, in any picture: in the moment we see depicted, it has not yet happened. In the picture, we smile because we do not yet know that things can get worse. Or we cry because we do not yet believe they can get better.

A photograph is thus rich in pathos, freighted with existential payloads, vibrant with meaning – or with deception. Each one is a *still*: a single image taken from the voluminous shadow play of experience. In the still we find, indeed, a certain stillness, a space in which (as Cavell says) thought is possible. Even the athletic action shots you will find in the following pages, which would seem to be antithetical – Ethel Catherwood in mid-high-jump in 1928,

Jackie Robinson sliding home at Montreal's Jarry Park in 1946 – acquire a tranquility, a gorgeous calmness, that invites reflection.

Moving pictures can startle and transport, and they are often more momentous and ceremonial than their time-stopped counterparts. Certainly more people go, more often and at greater expense, to see moving pictures than to view still ones. But only the still image has these poignant, world-deploying possibilities, this demand for reflection. Only the still image surrounds us so blithely, part of life's furniture, a thought waiting to happen.

4. Visions We cannot know all the shutter speeds employed by the many photographers included here, some of them anonymous and many of them long dead. We cannot know their motives, or their prejudices. But let us assume, for a moment, that each camera's shutter was open for an average of one-tenth of a second. That means that, together, these images constitute something less than a minute of actual elapsed time. These fractioned seconds limn the shape of 100 years, the growth of a country out of its infancy, the strife and unrest and disputes that make up so much of public life, but also the beauty and leisure and humour that leaven our time here.

The earliest photographs in this book, indeed the bulk of them, are the product of photojournalism, the documentary attempt to record a nation's activities. The very latest ones – a prime minister clutching a protester by the neck, another protester being helped to wipe the RCMP's pepper spray out of her eyes – are "screen grabs," television images that have been captured as stills from the electronic flow. In between there are candid shots and posed ones, professional portraits and amateur snaps, all the concrete work of the ever-present camera.

The reason for this range is clear. Photography is no longer the primary means of documenting the day-to-day events of the nation. But I think these grabbed images are the more powerful for being so grabbed, and they force us to consider the power of the still again. The single image stops your eye in a way impossible for the television replay, which simply repeats itself over and over until a kind of seamless banality is achieved, the images themselves rendered forgettable in the constant flow.

Photography emerges as a medium almost after the fact, an aesthetic arising out of its concrete applications rather than existing prior to them. In the beginning there is both excitement and discomfort about the camera's possibilities. The military display of war photographs, for example, complete with an image of two soldiers holding a human skull, appears not long after an early attempt at portraiture by Sidney Carter, itself not far removed from a newspaper shot of the bathing beauties of 1926, with their marcelled hair, knee-rolled stockings, and (by today's standards) surprisingly rounded tummies.

Inside the technology of the camera, technology itself is often at issue, from the otherworldly deep-water diver of 1905 to the muscular Hawker Sea Fury powering up on board the HMCS *Magnificent* in 1954. Even images of infrastructural disaster, such as the Kelly Block in Winnipeg covered in ice after a winter fire in 1911, have a sublime beauty.

There are dark images, too, from the public hanging in the century's first decade, to the procession of hearses bearing the women slain in the Montreal Massacre of 1989, to Karla Homolka's famously demonic visage in 1993. Conflict marks the century, both abroad and at home: labour riots in Winnipeg in 1919, a fight between Mounties and strikers in 1938, flag protests on Parliament Hill, kidnappings, murders, and soldiers in the streets of 1970 Montreal, violent student protests in 1997 Vancouver.

Simple posture can speak volumes. Marilyn Bell, pulled exhausted from the open water in the 1950s, has the heroic proportions and eloquent body language of a classical sculpture, agony in three dimensions. The 1920s Winnipeg Elk's Band spread their spindly Jazz Age limbs in a dozen crazy angles that together chart the exuberance of an ephemeral interwar moment. The Prince of Wales, leaning against a train during a Canadian visit in 1927, conveys shy elegance and sartorial perfection in perfectly cut suit and straw boater, but his body language is stiff, almost jittery. Mordecai Richler, by contrast, young and handsome in 1950s Montreal, sports a loose, world-beating confidence – and a truly superb haircut.

Other images have the sad beauty of time's traps. We see the cool-guy bell-bottoms and signature lapel rose of Pierre Trudeau, the belted overcoat of his wife, Margaret, as they happily swing their cherubic son Sacha in the Vancouver airport – future rifts and defeats and family death all unimagined, all unacted. Alan Eagleson and Ken Dryden, groovy in wide lapels and big-knot ties, share a joke that neither would probably remember by the time Eagleson was on the run from the law two decades later. And see Queen Elizabeth's slim grace, resplendent in her full-skirted dress and smart little hat, as she opens the St. Lawrence Seaway in 1959, never suspecting the trying future that would come to her family in the 1990s.

5. Longings It is impossible for such images not to bear a load of nostalgia, of course, to be subject to distortion and desire. There is no disclosure of the world free of bias or cost.

Nostalgia, the longing for what never was but should have been, is always created by technologies of representation. Nostalgia is a form of fantasizing, of daydreaming, about a mythical past captured – really, we should say *invented* – by a particular way of looking. The very same thought that the still image makes possible also opens up a space for certain kinds of emotion: an obscure sense of loss, a painful awareness of life's transitoriness, a sharp, irrational wishing to be elsewhere. ("A photograph," remarks a character in Proust's *Remembrance of Things Past*, "acquires something of the dignity which it ordinarily lacks when it ceases to be a reproduction of reality and shows us things that no longer exist.") Nostalgia is always about the present, about what we long for now, in the shadow of the past.

So I look at the 1964 photo of a cocktail party at the Place des Arts in Montreal and I wish the man depicted, flanked by two apparently identical Bond girls in floor-length white dresses, was me. I gaze into the face of a football player, caught in repose at a game in the early years of the century, and wonder what has happened to a world so simple, so perfect, that it made such a man, with his brave, direct countenance and mud-stained uniform. The Canada Pavilion at the 1939 World's Fair has such charming art deco lines and elegant type design that I wish, for a moment, I was among the crowds shuffling in. Hundreds of widows gather at the Vimy Ridge Memorial in 1936, all in proto-groovy sunglasses and berets, and an ineffable sadness seems to rise from the page to my eyes.

Some nostalgia is more proximate, and more genuine. For each one of us, some of these images will be suffused with smells and sounds, little virtual reality generators in two dimensions. Each one of us will have different points of entry to the country's century.

Gilles Villeneuve in his helmet in 1979, a racing hero when Canada had so few, later to die in a race and pass the torch to an even more famous son, takes me right back to Montreal and the first Formula One race I ever covered as a sports reporter. The deafening whine of those thoroughbred engines hits me, the giddy smells of high-octane fuel mixed in with hot dogs and popcorn and beer.

Yousuf Karsh, sitting in his studio in 1957, transports me abruptly to a living-room floor in the west end of Winnipeg, the Beatles' *Abbey Road* on the cabinet stereo, my father's *Atlantic Monthly*s spread across the floor, with their classified ads for "Karsh of Ottawa, Portraits," and me wondering if that could possibly be – no, how could it? – our Ottawa, *my* Ottawa.

I see a picture of a Woolworth's lunch counter in the 1950s, and all of a sudden I can precisely and vividly smell the grilled cheese sandwich and sweet pickle I used to eat with my mother at an identical one located in downtown

Summerside, Prince Edward Island, circa 1973. I smell her perfume, her hairspray, the leather and lipstick scents of her purse.

6. Belongings A nation, like a life, is a mixture of fact and fantasy, of vivid memories that turn out to be mistaken and keen desires to return to something you never had. It is all the hard daily detail of living: dressing ourselves, preparing and eating meals, going to work, finding time to relax, painting the many shades of workaday meaning.

Was this Canada's century? I said this book was not going to answer that question, but in one important sense the answer is obvious. This was my century, and it was yours. Like everyone who experienced even a small part of this stretch of time, of this nation, we helped make the world. *Of course* the century belongs to us.

Here is our world – 500 worlds – in black and white and colour. Listen to the thoughts they make possible.

Mark Kingwell

1909

Our 20th Century

"We didn't bring much more than the blessing the priest gave us as the carts went out of the old village. We'd auctioned the family goods and sold the farm to my nephew. We had a letter from a cousin who had gone ahead, and some advice from the Canadian who had come looking for settlers.

"When the ship docked at Montreal, Mother showed the government men we had savings, showed an address from my cousin who might still be expecting us. Then we got the families into the railroad car, Canadian Pacific Railway. Everyone squirming on wooden seats all day, unfolding our berths behind the canvas curtains at night. For two days and nights we crossed a farmer's nightmare, a forest large as Russia, endless lakes and rocks and trees. Kids crying and fighting up and down the cars.

"The train steamed into a city at dawn, Winnipeg. I heard two men talking a language I had thought I would never hear again: ours. We rolled on, crossing a plain broad as the ocean. There were wheat-field islands in seas of grass and fresh-baked villages rising along the railway track. The land looked like the poster we had seen back home, the one that said 'The Last Best West.'

"When the conductor told us this was our stop, we got out at a station with a few wooden buildings beyond. Hearts in the throat. We found the cousin I hadn't seen in six years, and I hadn't liked him much then. There he was with a farm, a wife now, kids. He poured a drink and told us it was true, what we heard back home. Free land, 160 acres. Break the soil, he said, plow it, plant it, build the farm. And it's yours — more land than ten families have in the old country.

"There were other people from the old country in the district, he told us. Even a priest was coming, and a teacher. So we led the families down the road to our places. And we stayed. Started working. Worked all the time."

Not every immigrant family came out of eastern Europe to the prairie West. Most came from Britain, the place Canada favoured, the place where Canada's agents recruited most enthusiastically. A few came across the Pacific from China and Japan and paid a head tax of $500.

But it would be the "Last Best West" people remembered. Ten million new acres of wheat in barely a decade. Close to a million new people on the prairies. Canada as the new breadbasket of the world. A stylish prime minister accepted a knighthood from Queen Victoria and uttered the first great quotation of the new era: "The 20th century will belong to Canada."

If you were that newcomer to the West in the century's first decade, you didn't at first know much about where you were. But home seemed to be growing up around you, people always coming, filling in the district, helping support the church and the school and the wheat pool.

There was talk that people like you were mongrelizing British Canada. Lads from your church got into some fights. But you built that good solid farm. You took off a crop each fall and got a price you could live with at the elevator. Your kids taught you to read the Eaton's catalogue and some of the grain growers' newspaper. Those people who said you didn't belong here must be wrong. You belonged to Canada. Belonged to the 20th century.

Visions 1900–1909

1900 June Welsh immigrants on board the ship that would take them to Canada.
At the beginning of the 20th century, the Dominion of Canada mostly comprised a vast
land rich in potential but poor in people. Wilfrid Laurier, the country's first French-
Canadian prime minister, handed the job of attracting immigrants to his minister of
the interior, an energetic Manitoban named Clifford Sifton, who described his ideal
immigrant thus: "a stalwart peasant in a sheepskin coat, born on the soil…with a stout
wife and a half-dozen children."

1900 August This panorama of a herd of 2,200 ewes grazing on untilled prairie conveys
a deceptively bucolic impression of the "Last Best West." Sifton's aggressive promotion
of Canada abroad helped set off a population explosion – especially in the prairies. What
would later become Saskatchewan held fewer than 100,000 people in 1900. By 1910
the figure would be close to 500,000.

Conditions were harsh for the settlers, most of whom arrived with few possessions. As one of those "stalwart" newcomers recalled it, the first winter was the hardest: "I don't know how we did it. All we had to live on was oatmeal, tea and rabbits."

1900 February to August The South African War, or Boer War (1899–1902), entered its second year. At the Battle of Paardeberg in late February, the Royal Canadian Regiment contributed significantly to this first British victory, after which the Imperial forces had the Afrikaners on the run. *Top:* Canadian troops pedalling to war on the War Cycle, a contraption designed to run along a railway track and to be used for scouting, sending dispatches, and ambulance work. *Above:* In April, members of Canada's Garrison Artillery helping defend the Modder River Bridge.

This photograph, with the title "The Dying Bugler's Last Call," must have been posed for patriotic home consumption. Support for the war remained strong in English Canada, but Quebec nationalists, led by Laurier's erstwhile ally Henri Bourassa, were vehemently opposed. One of the most famous regiments born during the Boer War was Lord Strathcona's Horse, entirely funded by Lord Strathcona, the man who had driven the last spike of the Canadian Pacific Railway. (In 1999, Lord Strathcona's Horse would be among the NATO contingents in Yugoslavia.)

1901 March The population of what would in 1905 become the province of Alberta reached 73,022. Like those pictured here, many settlers adopted the indigenous housing style for temporary accommodation, while in the cities of the East, capitalists amassed fortunes and built massive mansions. But wealth was already moving west. Winnipeg, a booming transportation hub, soon boasted more millionaires per capita than any other city in Canada.

1901 April Change the white frocks to dour black, and the guests at this wedding in Liverpool, Nova Scotia, could have been mourners at the funeral of Queen Victoria. Victoria's death at the beginning of the year and the beginning of the century marked the end of a record-long reign but not of Canadian fascination with British royalty. When the Duke and Duchess of York (the future King George V and Queen Mary) arrived for a royal tour in September, the whole country turned out to greet them.

1901 October Miss Annie Edson Taylor, age 63, became the first person to survive the trip over Niagara Falls in a barrel. After her feat, Miss Taylor, a dancing teacher whose business needed a boost, proclaimed: "I've done what no other woman in the world had nerve to do." The falls had been attracting daredevils since the 1850s, when it first became a tourist destination, but in the century's first decade such incidents multiplied. In 1912, stunting would be officially outlawed.

1902 March Monsieur S. LaCroix receiving a priest's blessing before his hanging as onlookers on power poles and rooftops watch the last public execution in Canada. The country's first professional hangman, John Robert Radclive, stands at the right. Radclive, who had once hanged a man already dead, grew increasingly haunted by his job. "The remorse which comes over me," he confessed, "is terrible and my nerves give out until I have not slept for days at a time." Canada's last execution took place at Toronto's Don Jail in 1962.

1902 June These women textile workers in Toronto most likely earned about half of what a poorly paid man did in 1902. "Equal pay for equal work" didn't exist as a concept in the century's first decade. Yet a surprisingly high proportion of the female population worked outside the home. In 1902, women made up approximately 13 percent of the total labour force, and many textile manufacturers depended on the skilled labour of women. But among the middle classes, a woman rarely kept a paying job after she was married.

1903 October Workers and travellers on the 46-kilometre Kaslo and Slocan Railway admiring the spectacular view at Payne Bluff, British Columbia. The early 1900s saw a continuing boom in railway construction and railway speculation. In 1903 Prime Minister Laurier announced the National Transcontinental Railway, intended to be Canada's third continent-spanning line. (It was never incorporated, ran way over budget, and was eventually absorbed by the CNR.)

1903 Winter Klondike prospectors started heading home. Their efforts in the gold fields (*top left*) were no longer panning out. Although Canada remained heavily dependent on the extraction and export of raw materials, new industries including tourism were already developing. The first Banff Springs Hotel (*top right*), built to lure tourists to the Canadian Rockies and provide extra revenue for the CPR, had been joined by 13 other railroad hotels from coast to coast.

1903 Summer A fisherman unloading his salmon catch. Teeming salmon stocks easily supplied West Coast canneries with enough fish for almost half a million cases in 1903. But salmon was only one of the many natural resource products that fed the economic boom. Even more important were prairie wheat (*top left*) and Maritime timber. Newly paved macadam roads such as Mount Pleasant Avenue in Saint John, New Brunswick (*top right*), were improving the comfort of urban travellers.

1903 October The Alaska Boundary Dispute was settled in favour of the Americans, with the entire Alaskan Panhandle awarded to the United States. The deal triggered anti-British protests because the sole British member of the boundary commission had sided with the U.S. Canada's sovereignty over its vast northern territories remained problematic for many more years. These pictures of Inuit life were taken during Albert Peter Low's 1903–04 expedition to the western shore of Hudson Bay, one of a series of Canadian expeditions intended to assert sovereignty in the Arctic.

1903 May Twenty-eight Doukhobors were arrested and charged with nudism near Yorkton,
North-Western Territory (now Saskatchewan). This year saw some of the first nude
protests by the Sons of Freedom, a radical splinter group of Doukhobors, a heretic sect
of Russian orthodoxy. (Their nakedness symbolized rejection of material things.)
The Canadian Doukhobors, who had fled Tsarist oppression, demanded control over their
own education and refused to swear allegiance to the Crown. The protests started soon
after the arrival in Canada of their Russian leader, Peter Veregin.   41

1902–03 Winter A team of Scottish curlers toured Canada and lost more matches than it won. By early in the century curling was one of Canada's most popular pastimes, as this Notman photo of a Montreal bonspiel suggests. During a tour of Scotland in 1908, Canadian curlers won 23 of 26 matches, including all three games for the first Strathcona Cup. Quebec women competed for the Coronation Cup as early as 1902, but the first national championship for women had to wait until 1961.

1904 April France gave up its right of access to the French Shore, the long sections of the coast of northwestern Newfoundland where French fishermen had held the right to dry their cod catches since 1763. *Above:* Dried cod being weighed at a merchant's scales in St. John's.

1904 September Students at an Alberta native school run by the Canadian-Anglican Mission. Intended "to better the lives of native children," these institutions banned aboriginal languages and isolated their students from native cultures to speed their assimilation.

1905 Summer These finely turned out Vancouverites hadn't waited for the Lord's Day Act of 1907, which would designate Sunday a statutory day of rest, to enjoy a scenic Sunday stroll in the Capilano Canyon.

1905 May Better diving costumes allowed workers to be employed cleaning and repairing ship bottoms. John Boyd, who took this photograph, was fascinated by the look of technology.

1905 August On land, child labour was prevalent – which accounted for such common sights as girls washing city steps (*right*). In the Nova Scotia collieries, the young sons of miners were apprenticed to their fathers. Not until 1929 did legislation prohibit most Canadian children from working in mines and factories.

1905 August At Fort Albany, native families (*top*) waiting outside the tent (*above*) where the signing of Treaty No. 9 between the federal government and the Cree and Ojibway of northern Ontario took place. The treaty extinguished aboriginal claim to an area one-third the size of the province in exchange for a paltry annuity and a reserve of 136,000 hectares abutting the shore of James Bay. With many native bands reduced to dependency by the decline of the fur trade, they were in no position to strike a hard bargain.

The signing was sealed with the exchange of gifts: for the Cree and Ojibway, beads and other trinkets. Treaty No. 9 was only the latest in a series of sweeping land claims settlements that paved the way for northern development. As one of their chiefs told the commissioners, "We are very poor and weak...Therefore in our hearts we thank thee, very much...Thou hast helped us in our poverty."

1905 June This photograph by Sidney Carter, founder of the Toronto Camera Club, is a rare early example of the camera used as an aesthetic tool. At the turn of the century, the pictorialist movement struggled to validate photography as an art. Pictorialists deliberately manipulated the pose of an anonymous subject and adopted diffused focusing to create a particular atmosphere. The camera was moving from a mere copier of the visual world to a means of artistic expression.

1905 July The Dominion Act created the new provinces of Alberta and Saskatchewan, bringing the total to nine running continuously from the Atlantic to the Pacific. Provincial status both recognized and fed the settlement boom. Men like this one waited all night outside the Dominion Lands Office in the new capital city of Regina in order to secure the quarter-section (160 acres, or 65 hectares) of land that would make their fortune. The land grant cost $10 but could be revoked if the settler failed to clear and cultivate the terrain.

1905 Summer Emily Carr, here standing in the garden of the House of Small, had yet to hit upon the evocative post-Impressionist painting style that would earn her fame if not fortune. When Carr's painterly quest began to take her into the forests and native villages, she at last found a sense of home: "It was as if everything hugged me," she later wrote, while in Vancouver it was "as if everything hurt."

It was not until she was in her late 50s that she began producing the mature work that caught the eye of members of the Group of Seven, who included her in a national exhibition in the late 1920s. But she remained a recluse to the end of her life. According to her biographer Maria Tippett, "Emily's companionship with animals not only fulfilled a lifelong need, but was a satisfying substitute for human relationships."

1906 May The Ontario government created the Hydro-Electric Power Commission of
Ontario, the first publicly owned electrical utility in Canada. Ontario Hydro would own
and operate the giant hydroelectric dam being built at Niagara Falls (*opposite, lower left*)
as well as the 12,000-volt transmission lines (*above*) that would carry electricity to
the towns and cities of southwestern Ontario.

Other enduring Canadian institutions were already well established. The Canadian Bank of Commerce had branches in frontier towns such as Vegreville, Alberta (*top*), and Dawson City, Yukon. But the brain drain had already begun. Alexander Graham Bell (*above right*), seen here lecturing on the principles behind the tetrahedral kite, had moved to the United States to develop his invention the telephone. But he still spent his summers at his estate near Baddeck, Nova Scotia.

1906 August A workman adjusting the upper cord eyebars of the cantilever arm of
the first Quebec Bridge, intended to link the city of Quebec with the south shore of the
St. Lawrence and to carry the National Transcontinental Railway across the river.
The design for the world's longest steel cantilever bridge, by the Phoenix Bridge Company,
was believed to be the "best and cheapest" plan. The work officially began in 1900.
The decade 1900–1909 saw an explosion of public and private works from coast to coast
in response to growing population and the expanding economy.

1907 June The Quebec Bridge collapsed into the St. Lawrence River, killing 75 workers and seriously delaying its completion. The bridge collapsed a second time in 1916, killing 10 more. It was not finally completed until 1917. Inevitably, in such a rapidly developing country, setbacks were bound to occur. In May 1902, a blast at the Coal Creek mine in Fernie, British Columbia, killed more than 125 coal miners. In November 1909, a train carrying Japanese workers on their way to repair a railway track crashed through a bridge into the Brunette Creek in Sapperton, B.C., killing 30.

1907 Spring Marquis wheat, an exceptionally hardy, early-maturing hybrid that Canadian government scientists developed by crossing Red Fife with Hard Red Calcutta, was for the first time planted widely in the Canadian prairies. It immediately proved its worth. Because of a later summer frost, many prairie wheat crops would fail that year, but the test fields of Marquis wheat survived. *Above:* A growing prairie family celebrates a bountiful crop.

1907 September Japanese merchants outside a Vancouver storefront wrecked during an anti-Japanese riot. The vast majority of European Canadians believed that people of Asian origin were inferior and impossible to assimilate. William Lyon Mackenzie King wrote in 1908, as deputy minister of labour: "That Canada should remain a white man's country is believed to be not only desirable for economic and social reasons but highly necessary on political and national grounds." Following the Vancouver riots, the Canadian and Japanese governments agreed to limit future Japanese immigration.

1909 April More than 2,000 Alberta coal miners walked off the job in a bid for collective bargaining rights and better wages. Miners, like the Saskatchewan miners pictured above, worked a 12-to-13-hour day, seven days a week. But the fledgling trade union movement was diffuse and disorganized, and most workers, like these British Columbia loggers (*left*), lived in the Dark Ages as far as their rights were concerned.

In 1900, the federal government had passed the Conciliation Act, which led to the founding of the Department of Labour. During the first decade of the 20th century the department mostly sought to encourage disgruntled factions to moderate their demands and to discourage production halts and slowdowns.

1909 December The University of Toronto defeated the Toronto Parkdale Canoe Club by a score of 26–6 in the first Grey Cup. The game's star was Smirle Lawson (carrying the ball, *right*). This early photo (*top right*) illustrates the uniform of the era. Throughout the decade, Canadian athletes made their mark. In 1906 Tommy Burns (*top left*), born Noah Brusso, became the first Canadian to win the world heavyweight boxing title, in a 20-round decision. And a Montreal policeman named Etienne Desmarteau (*above*) won Canada's first Olympic gold medal in 1904 in the 56-pound hammer throw.

1909 April Acadians raising a cross during an Easter observance in New Brunswick.
Canada was an overwhelmingly Christian country. Religion was part of the fabric of
everyday life, and sectarian differences, above all between Catholic and Protestant, ran deep.

1909 February At Baddeck, Nova Scotia, John Alexander Douglas McCurdy piloted
Alexander Graham Bell's *Silver Dart* in the first powered heavier-than-air flight in the
British Empire. *Right:* Two early Canadian aviation experiments.

Voices 1900–1909

The first chapter of the Imperial Order Daughters of the Empire (IODE) was established in 1900 by Margaret Polson Murray of Fredericton, New Brunswick, to promote Imperialism by supporting the war effort in South Africa. As the Empire waned, the IODE would use its considerable resources in support of education, immigration, child welfare, community health, and social services. Although a declining force, it remains an active women's organization in English Canada to this day.

The Original Aims and Object of the Order

1. **To stimulate and give expression to the sentiment and patriotism which binds the women and children of the Empire around the Throne and person of their Gracious and Beloved Sovereign.**
2. **To supply and foster a bond of union amongst the daughters and children of the Empire.**
3. **To provide an efficient organization by which prompt and united action may be taken by the women and children of the Empire when such action may be desired.**
4. **To promote in the Motherland and in the Colonies the study of the history of the Empire and of current Imperial questions...**
5. **To care for the widows and orphans and dependents of British soldiers or sailors and heroes during war, in time of peace, or under sickness, accident, or reverse of fortune...**

Imperial Order Daughters of the Empire 1900

As early as 1834, attempts were made to compose a national song for French Canadians. The most successful was "O Canada," written in 1880 by Sir Adolphe Basile Routhier, who later became Quebec's chief justice. "O Canada" was first performed in French on June 24, 1880, at the skaters' pavilion in Quebec City. It was not heard in English-speaking Canada until a literal translation was performed in Toronto in 1901, during a visit by the future King George V, when the anthem was received poorly. Montreal-based lawyer and writer Robert Stanley Weir then composed this original English lyric version, slightly altered by an act of Parliament in 1967.

O Canada

O Canada! Our home and native land!
True patriot love in all thy sons command.
With glowing hearts we see thee rise,
The True North strong and free;
And stand on guard, O Canada,
We stand on guard for thee.

O Canada! Glorious and free!
We stand on guard,
We stand on guard for thee,
O Canada! We stand on guard for thee.

Robert Stanley Weir 1901

Henri Bourassa resigned his seat in Parliament to protest against his party's decision to commit Canadian troops to the Boer War, fearing that Wilfrid Laurier had set a dangerous precedent. It was the beginning of a lifelong rift between the Liberal prime minister and his young admirer. Bourassa was the grandson of Louis-Joseph Papineau, Quebec hero of the Rebellions of 1837, but he espoused a gentler form of French-Canadian nationalism. In fact, his vision of a bicultural nation would become federal policy under Pierre Elliott Trudeau in the 1960s. The following text is a translation of a lecture Bourassa gave in Montreal in 1901.

Two partners **There are here neither masters nor valets; there are neither conquerors nor conquered ones: there are two partners whose partnership was entered into upon fair and well defined lines. We do not ask that our English-speaking fellow-countrymen should help us to draw closer to France; but, on the other hand, they have no right to take advantage of their overwhelming majority to infringe on the treaty of alliance, and induce us to assume, however freely and sponta- neously, additional burdens in defence of Great Britain. The Canadian soil, with its blood and its wealth, with its past, its present and its future, in short, our whole national inheritance is ours only to be handed down unimpaired to our descendants.**

*Henri Bourassa
1901*

In the terms of the century's first decade, Pauline Johnson was a superstar, a popular poet and a mesmerizing performer. The daughter of a Mohawk chief and an English mother, Johnson typically performed wearing the costume of an Indian princess. Her poetry drew on native tales for its subject matter while sounding cadences closer to those of Byron, Tennyson, and Keats.

Prairie Greyhounds C.P.R. **"No. 1," Westbound**

*Pauline Johnson
1903*

    I swing to the sunset land –
The world of prairie, the world of plain,
The world of promise and hope and gain,
The world of gold, and the world of grain,
    And the world of the willing hand.

    I carry the brave and bold –
The one who works for the nation's bread,
The one whose past is a thing that's dead,
The one who battles and beats ahead,
    And the one who goes for gold.

    I swing to the "Land to Be,"
I am the power that laid its floors,
I am the guide to its western stores,
I am the key to its golden doors,
    That open alone to me.

Canadian unity was Sir Wilfrid Laurier's great cause, one which he supported and defended throughout his 45 years in the House of Commons. He became Canada's first French-Canadian prime minister in 1896. During a campaign speech in Toronto's Massey Hall in October 1904, he uttered what would become his most famous words.

The century of Canada
I tell you nothing but what you know when I tell you that the nineteenth century has been the century of the United States development. The past hundred years has been filled with the pages of their history. Let me tell you, my fellow countrymen, that the twentieth century shall be the century of Canada and of Canadian development. For the next seventy-five years, nay for the next hundred years, Canada shall be the star towards which all men who love progress and freedom shall come. To those, sir, who have life before them, let my prayer be this: Remember from this day forth, never to look simply at the horizon as it may be limited by the limits of the Province, but look abroad over all the continent...and let your motto be: "Canada first, Canada last, and Canada always."

Wilfrid Laurier
1904

Clifford Sifton made his greatest impact as federal minister of the interior and superintendent general of Indian affairs in the government of Wilfrid Laurier, aggressively pursuing his agenda of strengthening the Canadian economy by encouraging immigration to the West. For thirty years he owned the *Manitoba Free Press* (now the *Winnipeg Free Press*), one of the most influential papers in Canada.

Within a single generation
We look forward to production of natural wealth of all kinds...We expect to see cities and towns springing up, in which the comforts and refinements of civilization will be within the reach of all. We expect to see a creditable system of education amongst our people, in which intellectual advancement and intellectual culture will go hand in hand with material progress. We expect another thing. We know that we have shown to the world that a western community is not necessarily a lawless community. But we hope to exhibit a great community, great in numbers and prosperity, built up within a single generation, in which respect for life and property is as profound, in which the administration of the law is as good as it is in the oldest and best organized communities of the world.

Clifford Sifton
1904

At the turn of the 20th century, reformers were busy addressing many social ills, not least the welfare of children. "Child-savers" attempted to improve living conditions for children through a number of means, among them legislative reform. The 1906-07 Ontario Legislative Assembly's Committee on Child Labour found that children as young as age eight had entered the labour force. Its report "Employment of Children and Young Persons in Canada" made numerous recommendations.

Hundreds of boys **Your committee recommend that provision be made forbidding the employment of children in such unhealthful occupations as acrobats, tumblers, etc. It has been represented to the Committee that in cities like Toronto hundreds of boys from nine to sixteen are frequent attendants at cheap shows. The late hours, nervous excitement and moral deterioration resulting from the practice are injurious to character. This with the reading of dime novels, smoking cigarettes, etc., frequently prevents boys from settling down to a trade or to regular employment, and leads to idleness, theft and vicious habits. Half the men in our prisons had, prior to conviction, never learned a trade. We, therefore, recommend that the attendance of children of either sex under fourteen years of age at theatrical and kindred performances when given by professionals should be prohibited, unless they are accompanied by parents or guardians.**

Ontario Legislative Assembly Committee on Child Labour 1907

Mark Twain called Anne Shirley "the dearest, and most lovable child in fiction since the immortal Alice." The audaciously eloquent heroine of Lucy Maud Montgomery's first novel, *Anne of Green Gables*, immediately captured the public's heart. Seven sequels and millions of copies later, it is still read and admired for its portrayal of Prince Edward Island and for its representation of female strength. In 1907, Montgomery described how she had created her most enduring character.

She took possession of me **I have always kept a notebook in which I jotted down, as they occurred to me, ideas for plots, incidents, characters and descriptions. Two years ago in the spring of 1905 I was looking over this notebook in search of some suitable idea for a short serial I wanted to write for a certain Sunday School paper and I found a faded entry, written ten years before: – "Elderly couple apply to orphan asylum for a boy. By mistake, a girl is sent them." I thought this would do. I began to block out chapters, devise incidents and "brood up" my heroine. Somehow or other she seemed very real to me and took possession of me to an unusual extent. Her personality appealed to me and I thought it rather a shame to waste her on an ephemeral little serial. Then the thought came, "Write a book about her. You have the central idea and character..." The result of this was "Anne of Green Gables."**

Lucy Maud Montgomery 1907

In 1903, Horatio Gilbert Parker was voted the fourth most important living Canadian in a poll conducted by the *Montreal Herald*. Sir Wilfrid Laurier, Sir Charles Tupper, and Lord Strathcona placed first, second, and third. At the time, Laurier was in his 60s and Tupper and Strathcona were in their 80s, and all three had played important roles in the politics of the emerging Canadian nation. Parker, on the other hand, was 43 and a backbencher in the British House of Commons. His fame in Canada came from his popular books. The following is taken from his highly successful 1909 novel, *Northern Lights*.

No more bull-wackers "You and your brother Bantry's got to go. This store ain't worth a cent now. The Hudson's Bay Company'll come along with the redcoats, and they'll set up a nice little Sunday-school business here for what they call 'agricultural settlers.' There'll be a railway, and the Yankees'll send up their marshals to work with the redcoats on the border, and –"

Gilbert Parker
1909

"And the days of smuggling will be over," put in the girl in a low voice. "No more bull-wackers and mule-skinners 'whooping-it up'; no more Blackfeet and Piegans drinking alcohol and water, and cutting each others' throats. A nice quiet time coming on the border, Abe, eh?"

The Canadian Pacific Railway, completed in 1885, made the flood of immigrants into the Canadian West possible. But it couldn't begin to provide the transportation infrastructure needed to support the mushrooming population. Between 1900 and 1910 branch lines proliferated and a railway building boom hit the prairies, as one of the contributors to Barry Broadfoot's *The Pioneer Years* remembered.

The railroad coming The thing I remember was the railroad coming.

Anonymous
circa 1905

There was every kind of men on the job you can remember and we highballed her. One man told me, a fellow who thinks he's a historian out at the university, he said that they put it through so fast that they were putting the tracks on the naked grass, right on the prairie, but that isn't so...But if old McArthur – he was from Winnipeg and in charge of the line, building from Winnipeg right on through – if he could have got away with it I think he would have. Man, he was a terror. A real terror.

We lived in tents and there wasn't a one I don't think that didn't leak...Some lived in cars, boxcars, and others just said to hell with it and made a tent with blankets and toughed it out that way.

Glory and Strife "The day war was declared was the proudest in my life. I went with my brother Charles to Father's office on St. James Street. All Montreal seemed to be cheering as the Montreal Scottish marched past. Charles in his uniform looked so young and brave, and the sun streaming in the window cast a special glow on him. I knew the fighting men, and we women at home, would make this world a better place. For Canada. For the Empire. For women. This was our war!

"Charles sailed with our Canadian Expeditionary Force in October. By spring they were at the front, at Ypres, and suddenly the casualty lists grew so long. So many of Charles's friends, and a young man I had been writing to. Soon we dreaded seeing a delivery boy with a telegram. And yet the German militarists persisted in their cruel folly.

"I threw myself into war work with the Imperial Order Daughters of the Empire, raising funds, running the soldiers' aid, and supporting the recruiters. Once a stuffy old captain at the armouries told us we should stay home and leave the war to men. 'Our husbands and brothers are at the front,' we said. 'Why aren't you?' That silenced him.

"Charles wrote of home and could I send more socks and chocolate and what good chaps the men were. But once, when he mentioned that one of our chums had been blinded, he added that his own life would be worthless anywhere but at the front. He was prepared to lay down his life for mankind.

"In time no one could imagine an end, and we just went on. We needed so many more men to complete the work. It made me furious to see the shirkers and slackers lounging about Montreal. Sir Robert Borden had promised half a million Canadians, but so many refused to serve King and Country.

"The brave French Canadians in the trenches understood our stake in the war. If we could not fight together for Christianity and civilization, how would we build our great country together after victory? But right here in Montreal, the mobs opposed conscription, and young men fled to the woods. I blamed the priests, and that awful Henri Bourassa, but even Sir Wilfrid Laurier put party ahead of the cause and refused to join Mr. Borden's great patriotic coalition."

In August 1914, crowds cheered Canadians who marched away for a quick, heroic victory. But the war struck every unresolved conflict in the Canadian fabric. Sir Robert Borden united English Canadians, both Conservatives and Liberals, behind his pro-war coalition, the Union government. French Canada revolted against Canada's enthusiasm for imperial sacrifice. Was Canada a nation or part of Britain's empire?

"I spent election day, December 17, 1917, canvassing for votes. Votes for women, and votes for conscription – how glorious it was! That night, I went with my sisters from the Montreal Suffrage Association, and we cheered ourselves hoarse as Sir Robert and our Unionist candidates swept to victory. I felt Charles was watching.

"For by then the telegram boy had come with that piece of paper, 'Regret to inform...' I scarcely know any living young men now."

Visions 1910–1919

1910 December Four members of the Royal North-West Mounted Police, led by Inspector Francis Joseph Fitzgerald, set out to take the winter mail from Fort McPherson to Dawson Creek, Northwest Territories. Despite Fitzgerald's experience at winter travel, his party lost their way, travelling 990 kilometres in 53 days but ending up only 56 kilometres from their starting point. All the members of the "lost patrol" perished. At the beginning of the decade, such a tragedy loomed large; by decade's end, it would seem but a pallid foretaste of deaths to come. *Above:* A Mountie garrison of the period.

1911 July Frustrated by a Conservative filibuster that had prevented passage of his recently concluded Reciprocity Agreement with the United States, Prime Minister Sir Wilfrid Laurier called an election for September. While free trade would dominate the campaign, other issues occasionally intruded, among them urban poverty, as exemplified by the Toronto slums (*above*). But there was little politicians could do about another social blight, the perennial threat of fire, such as the one that had destroyed Winnipeg's Kelly Block (*right*) that January.

1911 September The Conservatives, under Robert Borden, allied themselves with Henri Bourassa's nationalists in Quebec and swept the Laurier Liberals out of office with 134 seats to their 87. The campaign had pitted disgruntled English Liberals against their leader and protectionists against the economic continentalists, who believed that reducing tariffs with the U.S. would boost the Canadian economy, as Laurier's banners (*top left*) proclaimed. But with the country still booming, Canadians saw no need to open their borders to their rambunctious neighbour to the south.

Most voters were not impressed with Laurier's half-step towards creating a "tin-pot" Canadian navy. *Opposite, lower left:* A ship being laid down. Quebec nationalists denounced the navy as a colonialist commitment to the Empire; imperialists preferred direct contributions to Britain's Royal Navy, as promised by Borden. After his defeat, Laurier wrote, "I am branded in Quebec as a traitor to the French, in Ontario as a traitor to the English." *Above:* Laurier, holding his hat, on the campaign trail in Simcoe, Ontario.

SACRED
TO THE MEMORY OF
EVERETT EDWARD
ELLIOTT
OF THE HEROIC CREW
S.S. "TITANIC" DIED ON DUTY
APRIL 15, 1912.
AGED 24 YEARS.

EACH MAN STOOD AT HIS POST
WHILE ALL THE WEAKER ONES
WENT BY, AND SHOWED ONCE
MORE TO ALL THE WORLD
HOW ENGLISHMEN SHOULD DIE.
3.7

1912 April A gravestone for a crewman lost in the sinking of the *Titanic*. Edwardian faith in the human capacity to tame nature received a rude shock on the morning of April 15, 1912, with the news that the largest ship ever built had foundered off Newfoundland. Halifax earned the lugubrious distinction of being the port of return for the bodies recovered from the wreck and provided the graveyard for the remains of those whose families could not afford to transport them home.

In the years before World War I, the pace of progress must have seemed dizzying to a population mostly born before Marconi's wireless, Bell's telephone, or Edison's electric light. Already the automobile was evolving from an expensive and dangerous plaything (*top*) to an essential feature of Canadian life. But like the S.S. *Cheslakee* (*above*), which sank at Van Anda, near Powell River, British Columbia, technology new and old still had to contend with icebergs in one form or another.

1912 Summer At a race in Toronto, Tom Longboat (*above*, in the lead) set a world record for the 15-mile (24-kilometre) run. One of the most famous and successful of Canadian athletes in the pre-war years, Longboat was also controversial. A Mohawk from the Six Nations Reserve in Ontario, he battled both racism and racing orthodoxy. And when he ran in the 1908 London Olympics marathon, there were accusations of drug abuse. *Right:* In London, England, Prime Minister Robert Borden matched pace with young Winston Churchill, then First Lord of the Admiralty, as the threat of war with Germany grew.

1912 July Homeless residents surveying the aftermath of a killer tornado that left
28 dead and 2,500 homeless in Regina. A torrent of rain that followed quenched any fires
but made rescue operations muddy and perilous. Disasters, natural or otherwise, were
a feature of the building nation.

In the summer months, forest fires raged unchecked through vast stands of timber; in winter snowbound tracks caused nasty train derailments. In Calgary there were 380 fire scares in 1912 alone. With most city buildings still made of wood, an urban fire was just as devastating as a killer tornado.

1913 August The HMCS *Karluk* (*left*), on a scientific expedition to the Arctic under Vilhjalmur Stefannson, became trapped in pack ice off Camden Bay, Alaska. After the ship broke free, Stefannson spent the next five years discovering new Arctic islands while making the longest sledge journey on record. The decade witnessed considerable northern exploration. Scientists aboard the *Arctic* took seal specimens at Bylot Island (*top*), and the Canadian Arctic Expedition overwintered on Wrangell Island in 1914 (*above*), investigating the area's minerals, among other things.

1914 January Nellie McClung and other suffragettes held a mock parliament in Winnipeg to agitate for votes for women. In 1911, McClung (*above, right*) greeted the English suffragette Emmeline Pankhurst during her visit to Winnipeg. McClung and many other campaigners for women's rights belonged to the Canadian Women's Press Club, whose Winnipeg chapter (*top left*) was home to the Canadian suffragette movement. The movement was bolstered by temperance crusaders, such as these members of Calgary's Hillsdale Presbyterian Church (*top right*), who believed that liquor caused poverty.

Jobs for women mostly remained menial. Women worked at places like this Calgary baby clinic run by the Victorian Order of Nurses (*above*) or at home, but few had the help of the newfangled vacuum cleaner (*top left*). As for female education, girls were still taught in separate schools (*top right*). As McClung sarcastically remarked, "These tender-hearted and chivalrous gentlemen who tell you of their adoration for women, cannot bear to think of women occupying public positions...It is the thought of women getting into comfortable and well-paid positions which wrings their manly hearts."

1914 August Crowds of young men waited their turn at recruiting tents across Canada.
When Great Britain declared war on Germany, thousands raced to get in on a conflict that
many believed would be won before Christmas. Sam Hughes, Canada's minister of militia,
was a bombastic imperialist and enthusiastic amateur soldier whose chaotic recruiting
system was initially overwhelmed by volunteers. But after the first year of the slaughter,
recruiters had to scour the country.

By 1916, there would be close to half a million Canadians in uniform, but for much of the war Canadian troops would fight as part of the British army under British commanders. Of all Hughes's brainstorms, one of the saddest was foisting the inadequate but Canadian-made Ross Rifle on his troops. It performed so badly that many soldiers threw it away on the battlefield.

1914 October The First Canadian Contingent left for England. Before setting sail, raw recruits practised war drills, such as learning to tie knots (*top left*) and tend wounded (*top right*). For the families of the legions who would not return, posed pictures of men in uniform became talismans, such as the portrait (*above*) of members of the Hill Indian Colony Canadian Expeditionary Force smiling proudly beside tribal elders.

Photographers also caught fleeting moments like this farewell kiss as a troop train left the station. The First Canadian Contingent comprised a total of 33,000 men, 7,000 horses, and 144 pieces of artillery, making it the largest armed force to cross the ocean so far.

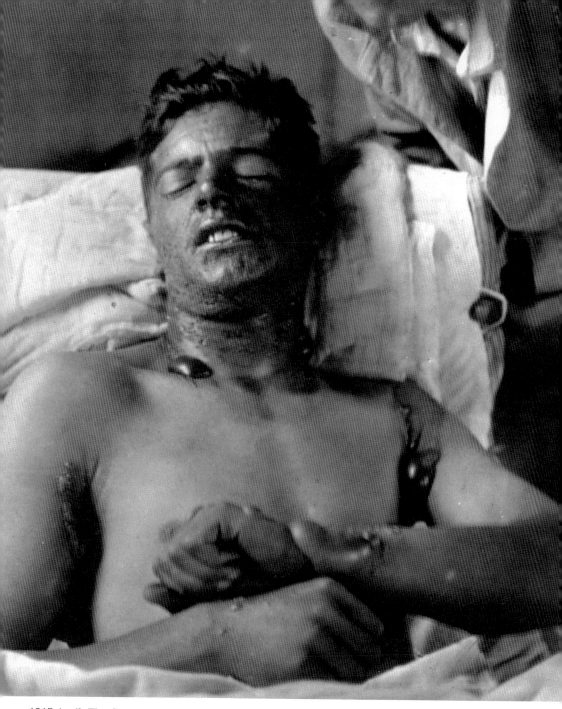

1915 April The Germans successfully used chlorine gas for the first time at Ypres, the bloodiest battle on the Western Front to date. The gas attack opened up a 6.5-kilometre gap in the Allied line, which was filled and held by the Canadian 13th Battalion at the cost of over 6,000 dead and wounded. Many soldiers in the Great War were badly burned by chlorine and mustard gas (*above*). Canada's most famous war poet, John McCrae, immortalized this sacrifice in his poem "In Flanders Fields," which described rows of white crosses in fields of red poppies. He wrote the poem in 20 minutes during the battle.

1915 November The first Canadian war loan, of $50 million, was issued. With much of the male workforce overseas, women took on non-traditional jobs, such as the assembly of airplane wings (*above*). Some cheap wartime labour was provided by the over 2,000 German prisoners of war sent to Canada, like those interned on the grounds of the Canadian National Exhibition in Toronto (*opposite, lower photo*).

So enthusiastic was the response to the first war loan that the amount was doubled by the end of the month, in part thanks to the patriotic exhortations of politicians such as Prime Minister Robert Borden (*top left*) and Premier William Hearst of Ontario. Silver Star Mothers (*top right*), women who had lost their heroic sons in battle, were paraded in front of admiring crowds.

1914–18 For the majority at home, life went on much as before. W. L. Mackenzie King, here standing between a Colorado miner and John D. Rockefeller (*top left*), was defeated in the 1911 election. He spent the war years in the United States, working as a labour consultant for Rockefeller, honing his mediation skills while serendipitously avoiding the looming conscription crisis. In St. Vital, Quebec, local swells found time to pose in a new water main (*top right*). In Alberta, oil exploration yielded some early gushers (*above*).

In the early years of the new century, a woman's hair was judged by its quantity and the elaborateness of its style, which meant that the coifs of upper-class women and girls, like this young Winnipegger (*top left*), would often be attended to by more than one maid. From coast to coast, Canadians continued to indulge their passion for summer camping (*top right*). And ice blocks still needed to be cut from the White Mud River (*above*) for use in summer refrigeration.

1916 October At Courcelette, France, Canadian infantrymen going "over the top" in a training exercise at trench-mortar school behind the lines. The autumn of 1916 saw the Canadians drawn into a gruelling campaign known as the Battle of the Somme, during which the Allies advanced a mere 13 kilometres over five months. In one of history's most vivid examples of military futility, the two sides lost almost 1.3 million men.

The huge sacrifice of 1916 helped convince Canada's top general, Arthur Currie, that throwing countless men at an entrenched enemy was ineffectual. He became a champion of the careful synchronization of artillery and infantry attacks. Pictures such as this one of German corpses littering the Somme battlefield served propaganda purposes. Almost invariably, photographs of Allied troops showed cheerful soldiers in immaculate battle dress, while the dead bodies belonged to the army of the evil Hun.

Borden's bill brings out the slacker and leaves your brother at home

1917 April Four Canadian divisions and one British under British general Sir Julian Byng (later Canadian governor general) launched an attack on Vimy Ridge. By April 14, they achieved their objective in the most decisive victory of the war so far. The previous summer, following Prime Minister Robert Borden's visit to the troops in France (*top left*), his Union government had passed the Military Service Act, making most men up to age 45 liable for military service. Borden's conscription bill was popular with veterans (*left*) and inspired recruiting efforts (*top right*) and graffiti (*above*) across Canada.

1914–18 Faces of war in France and Belgium (*clockwise from top left*): A crucifix greeted Canadians as they entered the town of Cambrai in November of 1917; a soldier sheltering from sniper fire; Newfoundlander Thomas Ricketts, who at age 17 was the youngest ever to win the Victoria Cross, the Empire's highest award for bravery in battle; a military chaplain conducting Sunday services from an aircraft cockpit.

Clockwise from top left: A youthful flier-in-training named Lester Pearson (he never saw combat) standing beside his airplane; air ace Billy Bishop in the cockpit of his plane; a soldier performing battlefield ablutions; two black soldiers resting during the loading of ammunition. The few blacks permitted to volunteer were assigned to a segregated non-combatant battalion.

1917 December Mourners at a mass funeral following the Halifax Explosion. Until the first atomic bomb was detonated, no human-made blast would be greater than the one that devastated Halifax in December – the worst disaster in Canadian history. Two ships – one a relief vessel, one carrying munitions – had collided, setting off a chain reaction that yielded an explosion a mile high. Sixteen hundred people died, and another 9,000 were injured, many of them blinded by flying glass.

The shock wave broke windows 100 kilometres distant, launched a tidal wave, and levelled much of the city (*top*), large sections of which were soon ablaze. Over 25,000 people lost their homes or suffered serious property damage. Burn victims (*above*) crowded hospital beds and overflowed into any other shelter they could find. For the first time, Canada's home front experienced the terror of modern weapons.

1918 August A group of Regina Boy Scouts doing their bit to support the war effort. Wartime expenses had forced the government to borrow heavily abroad and more heavily from its own citizens. In 1918, Canadians bought $600 million in Victory Bonds. Finally, by the late summer of that year, the tide of war had turned in favour of the Allies.

On November 11, the armistice brought an end to the fighting, but not to the war's far-reaching effect. A whole generation – one in 10 of Canada's 600,000 soldiers – did not return. But despite the sacrifice, Canada's showing in the fields of France fuelled national pride and independence.

1919 May–June The six-week-long Winnipeg General Strike, the largest outbreak
of labour unrest in the war's aftermath, paralyzed and polarized the city and triggered
a wave of (short-lived) strikes across the country. The most violent incident occurred
in Winnipeg on June 17 – Bloody Saturday – when Royal North-West Mounted Policemen
charged trade unionists (*above*), injuring 30 people and killing one.

The city divided down class lines, with anti-union rallies being organized by the well-heeled Citizens' Committee of 1,000 while poorer citizens marched in support of the strikers (*top*). When scabs tried to run a streetcar through a crowd, enraged strikers lifted it off its rails (*above*). Those in power characterized the strike leaders as "alien scum" and deported many of them. This fierce response helped squelch the drive for One Big Union to unite the Canadian working class.

1919 October A group of nurses in High River, Alberta, wearing face masks to ward off the Spanish influenza virus. The worldwide epidemic, carried and spread by returning soldiers, hit Canada hard. Of the 15 to 25 million deaths worldwide, between 30,000 and 50,000 were in Canada. When the epidemic peaked in October, some provinces banned public meetings and decreed that citizens wear gauze face masks out of doors. Many people feared to leave their homes at all and some communities enacted quarantines.

1919 June As leaders of the victorious Allied nations gathered at Versailles, France, wounded soldiers returned to Canada; however, the effects of the conflict would reverberate into an uncertain future. At the peace conference, Prime Minister Borden successfully insisted that Canada and the other dominions be separate signatories to the treaty, a clear and decisive step towards an independent Canadian foreign policy.

1919 January A group of invited dignitaries, posing amidst images of "the war to end all wars." An exhibition of Canadian official war photographs opened in London, England, and drew millions of visitors. The exhibition was billed as a display of "wonderful scenes of the battles of the Great War." According to the souvenir catalogue that accompanied the event, "the pictures portray striking incidents in the three months of glory through which Canadians fought without intermission from Amiens to Arras, and from Arras to the costly, but triumphant struggle for Cambrai."

Voices 1910–1919

One of the hottest political issues of the new decade was the naval question. The Liberal government's decision to build a small Canadian navy in response to Great Britain's call for help in building up its fleet drew sharp criticism from Imperialists, including Conservative leader Robert Borden. In January 1910, Borden gave a speech on the subject in the House of Commons, from which the following is taken.

This great empire How is it possible for any man in this country to imagine that Canada could be at peace with any great naval power in the world if that power at that very moment were at war with Great Britain? The thing is absolutely inconceivable. The nations of the British empire are separated by great stretches of ocean, the empire covers every continent in the world and these great nations are divided by vast distances, but upon the sea, any British navy, any Imperial navy, must be one. The jurisdiction and power of our government and of this parliament over expenditure and over control in time of peace must be maintained. I frankly admit that we must maintain that principle in view of our autonomy; but in time of war the naval force of Canada, the Canadian unit of the British navy, must be part of the British navy when engaged in the preservation and defence of this great empire.

Robert Borden
1910

Sir George Eulas Foster of the Conservative opposition joined the chorus denouncing Sir Wilfrid Laurier's reciprocity agreement with U.S. President Howard Taft. In English Canada, many prominent Liberals, including Clifford Sifton, attacked the deal. In Quebec, Conservative backing helped boost the *nationalistes* of Henri Bourassa. The combination handed the 1911 election to Tory leader Robert Borden, who campaigned on an anti-reciprocity platform.

The real reciprocity Dig your talc, and employ a few hundreds of men; send over the product of your pick-men and your shovellers to the United States, and let them do the perfecting processes upon it, and get the employment, get the accrued wealth, and get the national development. That is what [reciprocity] means. The part you call for Canada to keep is that which employs the least labour; what you give to the United States as the result of that employment of the least labour in raw material is what employs the greatest labour and runs up into the great figures of value which labour adds to the raw material in perfecting the product. The real reciprocity for Canada is the reciprocity between these different provinces. I put it to you, Sir, that if it were now 1867 and the provinces were asked to federate, with the alternative of free reciprocal trade with the United States of America, would we have any federation of these provinces? It would have been absolutely impossible.

George Foster
1911

In May 1914 the decrepit Japanese freighter *Komagata Maru*, carrying 376 Punjabis, most of them Sikhs, dropped anchor in Vancouver Harbour. Even though the would-be immigrants were all British subjects, they were refused permission to land and spent the next two months living in cramped, unsanitary conditions on the ship, while the Immigration Department sought a legal means of preventing their entry into Canada. Following is an excerpt from the *Vancouver Sun*'s coverage of the *Komagata Maru*'s arrival.

The greatest precautions

As soon as the Komagata Maru had been given pratique by Dr. Nemon, the quarantine officer, the steamer started for Burrard Inlet. It is understood that three immigration officers are on the steamer...As soon as daybreak came this morning many Vancouver Hindus collected on the waterfront in excited groups, talking in low voices, as if plotting schemes to aid their countrymen on the Japanese steamer to get ashore. The greatest precautions are about to be taken by the superintendent of immigration and his officers to prevent any of the Komagata's passengers from setting foot on shore.

The Vancouver Sun
1914

In 1914, John McCrae enlisted in the Canadian Expeditionary Force as a medical officer, having previously served as an artillery subaltern during the Boer War. His career as an author included several medical texts and a number of published poems. His most famous poem, "In Flanders Fields," written during the second battle of Ypres, was first published in the British magazine *Punch* in 1915. He died of pneumonia in 1918 at the military hospital he ran.

In Flanders Fields

In Flanders fields the poppies blow
Between the crosses, row on row,
    That mark our place; and in the sky
    The larks, still bravely singing, fly
Scarce heard amid the guns below.

We are the Dead. Short days ago
We lived, felt dawn, saw sunset glow,
    Loved and were loved, and now we lie
        In Flanders fields.

Take up our quarrel with the foe:
To you from failing hands we throw
    The torch; be yours to hold it high.
    If ye break faith with us who die
We shall not sleep, though poppies grow
        In Flanders fields.

John McCrae
1915

Throughout her lifetime, Nellie McClung campaigned on behalf of the temperance and suffrage movements, writing 16 books and numerous articles. In 1915, she and her family moved from Winnipeg to Edmonton, where she continued her active membership in the Liberal Party, subsequently gaining a seat in the Alberta legislature. The following text is from *In Times Like These*, a powerful evocation of McClung's lifelong struggle on behalf of the voiceless and the downtrodden.

A new chivalry Chivalry is something like the icing on the cake, sweet but not nourishing. It is like the paper lace around the bonbon box – we could get along without it.

Nellie McClung
1915

There are countless thousands of truly chivalrous men, who have the true chivalry whose foundation is justice – who would protect all women from injury or insult or injustice, but who know that they cannot do it – who know that in spite of all they can do, women are often outraged, insulted, ill-treated. The truly chivalrous man, who does reverence all womankind, realizing this, says: "Let us give women every weapon whereby they can defend themselves; let us remove the stigma of political nonentity under which women have been placed. Let us give women a fair deal!"

Louis Hémon was born in Brest, France, but he is primarily remembered for his classic tale of habitant life, *Maria Chapdelaine: Récit du Canada français*. Written while Hémon was living in the Lac-Saint-Jean region of northern Quebec, the novel celebrates the traditional culture of rural Quebec, already challenged by the urban and secular world. Upon completing the book, Hémon set off to explore western Canada but was killed in a train mishap in Chapleau, Ontario. *Maria Chapdelaine* was published in Montreal in 1916.

If you were my wife "This...this is no place for you, Maria. The country is too rough, the work too hard; merely to earn one's bread is killing toil. In a factory over there, clever and strong as you are, soon you would be in the way of making nearly as much as I do; but no need of that if you were my wife.

Louis Hémon
1916

I earn enough for both of us, and we should have every comfort: good clothes to wear, a pretty flat in a brick house with gas and hot water, and all sorts of contrivances you never heard of to save you labour and worry every moment of the day. And don't let the idea enter your head that all the people are English. I know many Canadian families who work as I do or even keep shops. And there is a splendid church with a Canadian priest as curé – Mr. Tremblay from St. Hyacinthe. You would never be lonesome..."

"I do not like to kick a man when he is down but I am willing to break nine toes in kicking Sam in the stomach or in the face or anywhere else." One soldier spoke for many upon learning in 1916 that Sir Samuel Hughes had been fired as militia minister. One of the most colourful figures of his era, Hughes's efforts as Canada's top military official were marred by scandals and marked by administrative incompetence. But he was not without his successes, as he had told Parliament earlier in 1916.

Noble service **Canada has developed confidence in her manhood, and confidence in her womanhood. The women of this country have performed noble service, perhaps even better than the men, and they continue to give great encouragement to the work that is going on. We have turned out 250,000 soldiers, who have already made an historic record in the world, and 100,000 skilled mechanics. Our manufacturers, at the present time are capable and ready for any undertaking. As I have said, at the outbreak of war, Canadian financial and industrial life was paralyzed. After making due allowance for the imported products which went into the shells made in Canada, there has been added to the wealth of Canada, through the action of the Shell Committee, $250,000,000; or $30 each for every man, woman, and child in the country.**

Samuel Hughes
1916

In May 1917, after visiting the Western Front, Prime Minister Robert Borden returned to Canada convinced of the urgent need for troop reinforcements. His Union government passed conscription legislation, but only over the bitter objections of every French-Canadian MP. In the end, mandatory military service did little to influence the outcome of the war: although more than 400,000 men were registered during the draft, only 125,000 became members of the Canadian forces and fewer than 25,000 actually made it to France.

Persons Liable for Service

An Act Respecting
Military Service
1917

(1) Every male British subject who comes within one of the classes described in section three of this Act, and who, –
(a) is ordinarily resident in Canada; or,
(b) has been at any time since the fourth day of August, 1914, resident in Canada, shall be liable to be called out as hereinafter provided on active service in the Canadian Expeditionary Force for the defence of Canada, either in or beyond Canada, unless he
(a) comes within the exceptions set out in the Schedule; or,
(b) reaches the age of forty-five before the class or subclass to which he belongs, as described in section three, is called out. Such service shall be for the duration of the present war and of demobilization after the conclusion of the war.

Ralph Connor did not set out to be an author, but after a Presbyterian magazine, *The Westminster*, published several of the young minister's fictional tales, he began a series of novels based on his shorter works. His first three books, which were popular accounts of adventure, courage, and morality, sold 5 million copies. The following passage is from *The Sky Pilot in No Man's Land*, Connor's most moving story of war.

Count me in "Count me in," said Tom Fielding quietly. "I have a wife and three kids, but –"

Ralph Connor
1917

"My God!" gasped Duff. "My wife." His face went white. He had not yet fully adjusted himself to the fact of war.

"Why, of course," said Mr. Howland, "you married men won't be called upon. You must be reasonable. For instance you, Mr. Duff, cannot leave your wife."

But Duff had recovered himself.

"My wife, sir? My wife would despise me if I stayed up here. Sir, my wife will buckle on my belt and spurs and send me off to the war," cried Duff in a voice that shook as he spoke.

With a single stride Barry was at his side, offering both his hands.

"Thank God for men like you! And in my soul I believe the Empire has millions of them."

As the decade drew to a close, eager advertisers boasted of the superiority of motor-driven contraptions over animal-drawn vehicles.

I am One of the Wonders of the World

I am the REIN-DRIVE TRACTOR.

Rein-Drive Tractor
advertisement
circa 1917

I have the strength of ten draught Horses...

No disease of foot or mouth can injure me. I suffer not from heat or cold. I wear no harness, at night turn off my spark of life and I will await your coming, however long.

When you are ready to work I am at your service, to do as you direct, without fear of whip or utterance.

When the day's work is finished for you, go rest yourself – stop my heart-beats for the time, or send another man to guide me, for I am never tired...

We will make a reputation for service to our people as great as our wonderful Army in France, for I, too, am a Canadian and ready to serve.

I am Tireless, Efficient and Economical.

I am the REIN-DRIVE TRACTOR.

I am the Real Iron Horse.

1929

Struggling Twenties

"I was always a lad who was good with his hands, I was. So when I came back from the war and got on at the coke ovens in Sydney, they always had me at repairing and fixing.

"Lord Jesus, now there was a hard place. I'll be on my deathbed and I'll remember those furnaces like the gates of Hell and the smoke in my eyes and nose. BESCO, that was the British Empire Steel Company, owned all the coal mines, and all the steel plants too. They owned us, near enough.

"We went out in 1923. The bosses had cut our pay packets by a third, no less. Well, we had to go out, didn't we? Who could live on that?

"The company cut off credit at the company stores. If you rented a company house and you were a striker – out! Good with the fists we had to be when the mainlanders sent the provincial police up to break strikers' heads. Then troop trains rolled in from up in Canada, machine guns mounted on the front! Weren't we just after fighting a war to keep this country free?"

"Roaring Twenties" was one of those phrases Canadians picked up easily from across the border. But for much of the 1920s, there was not much roar in Canada. Business contracted. More people left than arrived. Strikes erupted into class war.

The buzz of prosperity was first heard in British Columbia and Ontario. With timber and minerals and salmon to ship away to the world through the new Panama Canal, Vancouver blossomed. The towns of southern Ontario began to prosper. By the end of the decade, auto plants, all

American-linked and mostly in Ontario, had put a million cars on Canada's roads. Some Canadians even got a taste of stock market fever, and the fashion crazes, the flapper and the "New Woman." But it was not the roar of prosperity that sounded in everyone's ears.

"By the spring of '25, our strike fund was gone, and people were starving all over Sydney, Waterford, out to Glace Bay. Father Greg ran soup kitchens at the church hall. Our strike leaders, Red Danny Livingstone and the rest, were in jail. Tools of Moscow they were called. But still we stayed out.

"One of the bosses, McLurg by name, said it didn't matter how long we stayed out and starved. The workers would give in, he said. We couldn't stand the gaff, is what he said.

"Well, some of the lads decided to see what the company could stand. They put the torch to the power station up Waterford way that was keeping the mines pumped out. You could see Hell's own flames from a mile away. But the company police hurt us, too. One of ours, a right good lad my sister knew, got his head caved in, and he died there in the middle of the fight.

"But what McLurg said was true. Striking half our lives and out of work the other half – what were we standing it for? BESCO went bust in 1928, but the mines opened again, and someone else got the steel plant going.

"By then, I was fixing cars. Even in Sydney, some people were driving Model Ts and McLaughlins, and a man could make himself useful when he was good with his hands. Can't say that I missed the coke ovens any. No, sir."

Visions 1920–1929

1920 Summer Canada's early exports to Hollywood included Mary Pickford and a hero on horseback. This still photograph from *Cameron of the Royal Mounted*, filmed in Bankhead, Alberta, demonstrates that the Mountie is our earliest and most enduring screen image. By now this scarlet-suited, be-Stetsoned cliché figure has starred in hundreds of American movies – notably the treacly *Rose Marie* of 1936 – few of which owe any debt to accuracy.

1920 May The newly formed Group of Seven held its first group exhibition at the
Art Gallery of Toronto. Perhaps one of the graphic designers at work in the Eaton's
catalogue department (*top*) was a great artist in the making; after all, several members
of the Group of Seven, shown above at the Arts & Letters Club in Toronto, started
out as professional illustrators. *Clockwise from left front:* A. Y. Jackson, Fred Varley,
Lawren Harris, Barker Fairley, Frank Johnston, Arthur Lismer, J. E. H. MacDonald.

The Group of Seven established its reputation with rural landscape painting, despite the obvious graphic possibilities of scenes such as this Toronto stocking factory. Several members of the Group and its disciples tried their hand at portraiture, notably Varley, but you will look long and hard through their collected works for any sign of urban life.

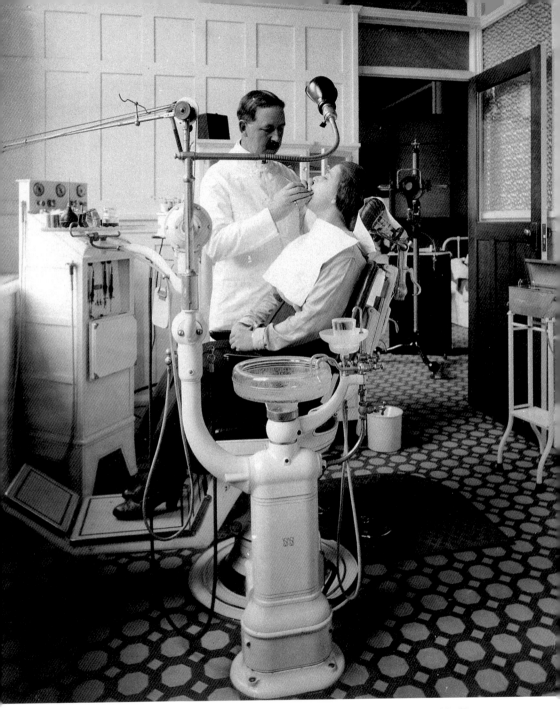

1921 September Frederick Classens of London, Ontario, invented a portable X-ray machine, only one of many technical advances that fed postwar improvements in public health. Those with money could visit dentists supplied with the latest equipment, but prosperity was slow to reach most regions of Canada outside Ontario and British Columbia.

Women who remained in the workforce had to settle for low-paying jobs, like these switchboard operators (*top*). Gradually, however, American investment and branch plants brought greater affluence and many material improvements. More and more automobiles filled the roads and some of the drivers were women, like the one in this Studebaker coupe near Cochrane, Alberta (*above*), a clear sign that social norms were loosening.

1921 January The "Made in Canada" cushion in this Eaton's interior (*above*) provides a suitable metaphor for the many Canadian institutions that began this year. In March, the Canadian Authors Association was founded, with Stephen Leacock as its first president. Also in March, the *Bluenose* (*opposite, top left*) took her maiden voyage from Lunenberg, Nova Scotia, the launch of a legendary racing career that lasted until 1939. In May, Frank Underhill and two other academics started the magazine *The Canadian Forum*.

In July, the United Farmers of Alberta won the provincial election, joining their Ontario brethren, who had thrown the reigning Tories out in 1919. On December 6, Agnes Macphail (*top right*) became the first woman elected to Parliament, the only woman to win a seat in the election that first brought William Lyon Mackenzie King to power. But traditions remained strong. During the summer, Ontario celebrated (six years late) the tercentenary of Samuel de Champlain's arrival at Georgian Bay (*above*).

1921 September In the 1920s Montreal (*left*) was indisputably the country's first city in population, economic clout, and cultural activity. But Winnipeg remained both a business and a cultural powerhouse and one of many cities where exponents of the new music called jazz, with its roots in vaudeville and ragtime, thrived, among them Elk's Band (*above*). Moralists decried the unseemly gyrations dancers performed to its syncopated rhythms, but the dancers just kept on dancing.

1922 August Strikers in Sydney, Nova Scotia, stoned a train carrying troops from Halifax. In response to a drop in world coal prices, employers such as the huge Dominion Iron and Steel Company, whose Sydney plant is pictured above, had cut pay and tried to crush the union. Wrote union leader James Bryson: "Brothers! War is on – a class war. There is only one way to fight, and it is to cut production...Up men in your organized thousands and attack them." Elsewhere more frivolous matters preoccupied the growing middle class, including this woman having her hair curled and set in an Eaton's beauty salon (*right*).

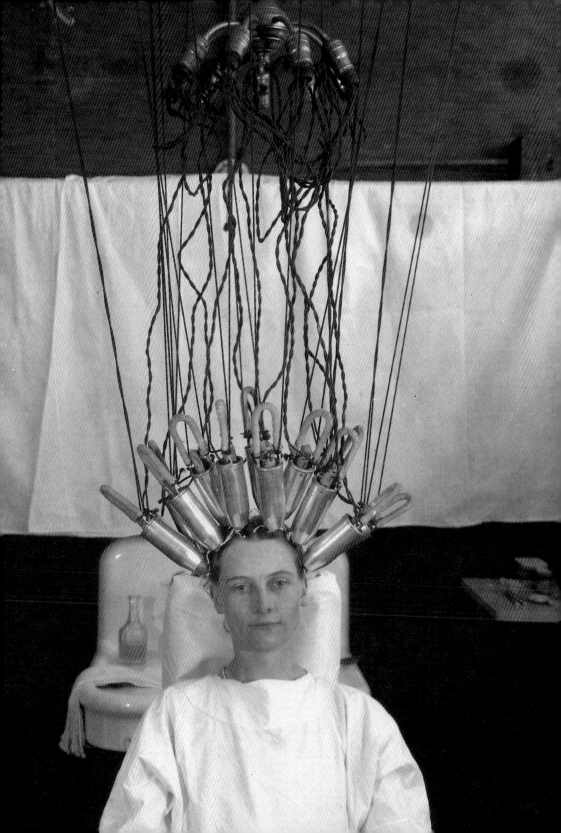

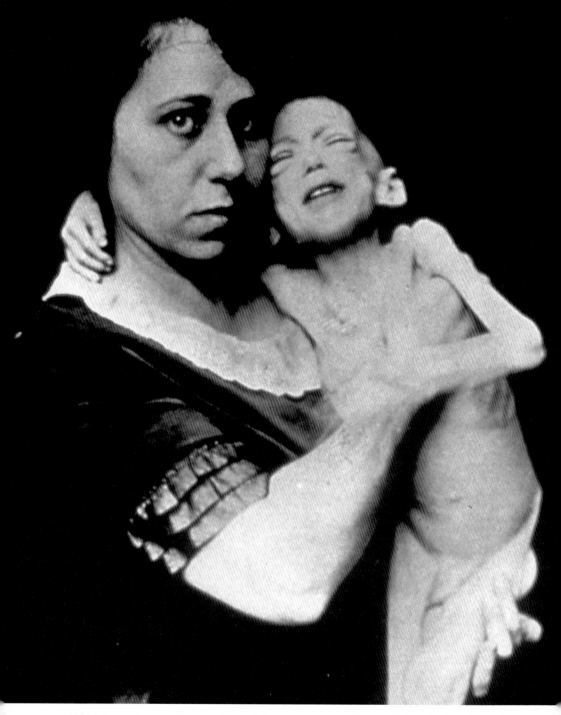

1922 March A team of researchers at the University of Toronto, led by Frederick Banting and Charles Best (*right*), announced the discovery of insulin. The breakthrough meant hope for juvenile diabetics such as "J. L. Age 3 years, weight 15 lbs" (*above*). The 1920s also witnessed considerable advances in pediatrics led by specialists such as Montreal's Alton Goldbloom, the first Jew to hold a Canadian university chair and one of the founders of the Canadian Paediatric Society in 1923.

1922 November The first Royal Winter Fair was held at the newly built Coliseum on the Canadian National Exhibition grounds in Toronto. From the beginning the fair drew agriculturalists from coast to coast and throughout the United States, who showed off their prize animals and prime produce. In its first year the fair exceeded even the most optimistic expectations, with more than 17,000 entries and over 150,000 visitors.

The FLYING BULL
WALDORF PRINCE ROYAL
WALDORF FARMS NO. CHATHAM, N.Y.

From the beginning, the Royal Winter Fair's highlight has always been the livestock, with a particular emphasis on horses, dairy cows, and beef cattle. But there were also national field crop competitions, promoting new varieties of wheat. In the early years, the show items invariably arrived by train. But in 1929 the celebrated "flying bull" (*above*) arrived in Toronto by airplane.

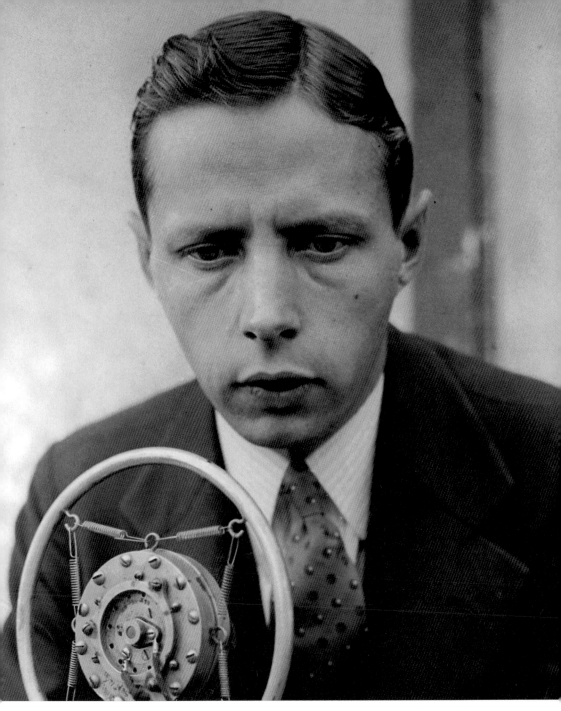

1923 March Nineteen-year-old reporter Foster Hewitt (*above*) ushered in the electronic sports era when he provided live play-by-play of a game between Toronto Parkdale and Kitchener on the *Toronto Star*'s new radio station, CFCA. It was only the third hockey game ever broadcast and the beginning of a career that made Hewitt into the "voice of hockey." When Maple Leaf Gardens was opened in 1931, it included a broadcast booth for the by then famous announcer. *Left:* Whether at the hockey rink or at the race track, women sported the latest flapper style.

1923 June Calgary's annual Agricultural Exhibition merged with an annual rodeo known as the Stampede to form the Calgary Exhibition and Stampede. The 1923 edition was a resounding success, attracting 123,000 people on its final night alone. Visitors enjoyed such highlights as chuckwagon races (*top*) and a street dance in downtown Calgary (*above*), and thrilled at the horse that dove 15 metres into a 3-metre-deep tank of water (*right*).

1925 October In the federal election, the Liberals won 17 fewer seats than the Conservatives, but Mackenzie King clung to power with the support of members of the Progressive Party and the Labour Party. Less than a year later, facing a certain vote of censure, King caused a constitutional crisis when he asked Governor General Lord Byng (*above*, meeting Crees in Edmonton on his first Western tour) to dissolve Parliament. Byng refused King's request and called on Conservative leader Arthur Meighen to form a government. It lasted only three days.

On the night of the ensuing election, Liberal supporters waiting outside the Winnipeg offices of the staunchly Liberal *Manitoba Free Press*. Along with legions more right across the country, they would celebrate another King victory. A few months later, "Byng of Vimy," the man who had led the Canadian Corps to victory at the famous World War I battle, retreated home to Britain. But his name remained on the hockey trophy for sportsmanship donated by his wife in 1925.

1925 October Hollywood's greatest early movie star, Toronto-born Mary Pickford, released *Little Annie Rooney*, a film for which she wrote the scenario and in which she played the title role. She hid her script work under the nom de plume Catherine Hennessey, the name of her beloved grandmother. Pickford, shown here with her husband Douglas Fairbanks, was the biggest box-office draw of the 1920s. She and Fairbanks were founders of United Artists, the first star-controlled production company.

1926 Summer Young women vying for first place in the first Miss Toronto contest at Sunnyside (*top*). Hardly imaginable in the days of Queen Victoria, in the 1920s bathing beauty competitions had no trouble attracting contestants or crowds. Such modern pastimes competed with more traditional public entertainments, such as the circus at Toronto's Dufferin Race Track to which these elephants (*above*) are luring passersby.

151

1927 July Crowds gathered in front of the Parliament Buildings (*top*) to celebrate the 60th anniversary of Confederation. Those who couldn't make it to Ottawa held local festivities and decorated public buildings, such as this Nova Scotia post office (*above*). The day also marked a milestone in Canadian radio history. A makeshift coast-to-coast network of 23 radio stations broadcast the Diamond Jubilee celebrations, which were attended by the Prince of Wales and his younger brother, the Duke of York (*right*).

1927 September In Vancouver, A. W. Neill, MP for Comox-Alberni, presenting Canada's first old age pension cheque (*left*). Mackenzie King had promised J. S. Woodsworth that he would enact pension legislation in exchange for the support of Woodsworth's tiny Labour Party in 1925. The cheque was for $20, about $200 in 1999 dollars.

1928 April In Montreal, New York Ranger manager Lester Patrick (*above*), age 44, replaced his injured goalie in the second game of the Stanley Cup Playoffs.

1928 October By the late 1920s Alberta was enjoying its first oil and gas boom, centred on the Turner Valley, known as "Little Chicago," where oil was first discovered in 1910. By the end of the decade, 10 different extraction sites were being operated by a variety of companies. But the real oil boom didn't sound in Alberta until February 1947, when Vern "Dry Hole" Hunter drilled a gusher at Leduc Hole No. 1.

1928 August Among the Canadians who excelled at the Amsterdam 1928 Olympic Games was Percy Williams, who won the 100-metre sprint (*top, in the middle*), garnering one of Canada's four gold medals in track and field. In the first Olympics that included women, Fanny Rosenfeld (*above left and right*) won a silver medal in the 100-metre dash and shared a gold medal with three other Torontonians in the 400-metre relay. After 19-year-old Ethel Catherwood (*right*), known as the "Saskatoon Lily," won gold in the high jump, the *New York Times* dubbed her "the prettiest of all the girl athletes."

1928 September This photograph, "The Family," by John Pearson Morris was one of 200 images chosen for the Third International Salon of Pictorial Photographers of America. As the photograph unwittingly implies, smaller families became the norm during the 1920s as the population steadily shifted from the country to the cities. (Already in 1921 almost half of Canadians lived in urban settings.) And while many women had returned to the joys and toils of home and hearth after the Great War, an increasing number combined child-rearing with a job outside the home.

1929 October The stock market crash on Wall Street caused panic on world markets, but the Depression in Canada had as much to do with wheat – the staple of the Canadian economy. In 1928 a world wheat glut had left millions of bushels of unsold grain rotting in prairie elevators. The wheat crash threw the Winnipeg Grain Exchange into a tizzy and triggered a down-spiralling domino effect in the Canadian economy. Not until the second half of the 1930s would grain prices recover and, with them, prairie agriculture.

1929 Summer Prairie farmers always worried about getting enough rain, particularly on the dry short-grass prairie known as Palliser's Triangle, in Alberta and Saskatchewan, which had experienced dust bowl conditions before. But the pandemic prairie drought began in 1929 and persisted, with periods of remission, until 1937. All too quickly, the endless fields of ripening wheat turned into deserts plagued by devastating dust storms.

As one farmer recalled: "Dust would cover up the fence posts and the farmers would come along with a wagon load of more poles and string another fence, on top of the first. I could never figure out why they did this because there were no cattle wandering at large; they had all been slaughtered long ago or taken to the community pastures. Farmers did funny things in those days. They still do, but everybody was just a little bit loco in that country then."

Voices 1920–1929

The Group of Seven – painters Franklin Carmichael, Lawren Harris, A.Y. Jackson, Frank Johnston, Arthur Lismer, J.E.H. MacDonald, and F.H. Varley – came together in 1920 through a common desire to escape the conservative limitations of most Canadian art of the time. The group's paintings broke from Canadian tradition by shifting away from imitation in a conscious effort to create a more subjective artistic reality. This statement by Lawren Harris outlines the mandate of the group.

Creative adventure in art
A group of young Canadian painters came together drawn by an irresistible urge to replace this "foreign-begotten technique" by a way of painting dictated by Canada itself, to concentrate all their energies on making a Canadian statement in art in Canadian terms...It meant that these young painters would be obliged to free themselves from every influence which might come between them and Canada as a new world for creative adventure in art. This, broadly speaking, was the motive force behind the "Group of Seven."

Lawren Harris
1920

Robert Chambers Edwards, publisher of the legendary *Calgary Eye Opener*, was surely the most colourful journalist of his era. He lampooned stuffed shirts and received opinions with equal relish – and he wasn't afraid to switch sides on an issue. In 1916 he supported prohibition in the Alberta referendum. But by 1920 he was singing a different tune.

Disgraceful orgies
Our views on the subject of prohibition have undergone considerable change since the memorable days when we worked so hard in favour of it. The whole thing has proved a farce...

Bob Edwards
1920

We have kept hammering away at these booze parties in the home for a long time now, with no tangible results outside of an occasional knowing wink, and smile from the cognoscenti. Everybody knows of the disgraceful orgies that are pulled off nightly in private homes along our quiet avenues which look so innocent, childlike and bland during the day. They form a favourite subject of cynical conversation amongst men during office hours.

If the women who participate in these debauches only knew how lightly their names are bandied about amongst the men downtown, they would surely pause and do some calm reflecting for their own sakes.

Women celebrated full federal enfranchisement in 1918 with the passage of the Women's Franchise Act, which not only gave women the vote but also allowed them to run for public office. By 1922, all the provinces had enfranchised women, except Quebec, which held out until 1940. W.E. Maclellan's words, written in 1921 during the first election campaign in which women were entitled to vote, make it clear that, even with full access to the vote, many still saw public life as a strictly male domain.

To elevate politics **Few mature women really desired the franchise. What good, then, has been done by this fine and radical extension of the franchise? It has simply doubled the electorate, without making it wiser or better or more discriminating. It has greatly complicated the election preparations. It has opened the door to far wider and more demoralizing corruption...it has wrought prospective evil in this; while many of the better class of women will not vote, no such abstention is to be expected from a less desirable class...The thing does not look pleasant or commendable just now, but it may improve on acquaintance. Let us hope so. Everyone, however, may as well awake from the dream that women are going to "elevate politics" by their votes or otherwise.**

W.E. Maclellan
1921

On October 31, 1920, after reading an article in a medical journal, Frederick Grant Banting made a note about a hypothesis for isolating a long-sought secretion from the pancreas. His idea was physiologically incorrect, but it led to research by a team at the University of Toronto that eventually yielded insulin and the Nobel Prize for medicine. Here Banting describes the striking impact of insulin on one diabetic patient.

Before and after **He was a very handsome man of 30 & he deposited in the easy chair 76 lbs of the worst looking specimen of a wife that I have ever seen. She snarled and growled and ordered him about. I felt sorry for him. I placed her in hospital more in pity for him than in regard for her.**

A year later I was at my desk early one morning when the phone rang. A cheerful chuckling voice asked if I would be there for ten minutes...In a few minutes I heard the outer door open and a moment later my office door was thrown wide open as in rushed one of the most beautiful women I have ever seen. She was a stranger. I had never seen her before yet she threw her arms around my neck and kissed me before I could move from where I stood. Over her beautiful head I saw the laughing face of the patient husband. I stood back. The three of us stood hand in hand. I looked at them. The husband said "Doctor I wanted you to see her now. This is the girl I married – before she had diabetes."

Frederick Banting
1922

The most famous sports call in Canadian history, "He shoots, he scores!" was Foster Hewitt's calling card. Much more than a broadcaster, Hewitt was a master performer with the ability to breathe life into a game. He broadcast more than 3,000 hockey games. But the first one in 1923 made one of his most vivid stories.

You're our man "I hope you're not suggesting anything strenuous, Basil. I'm beat. I've had a hard day. I'm all in."

"This isn't too hard, Foster. In fact it may pep you up. Anyway I can't avoid it. All plans are made. The notice is in the paper."

"What is it? Not another orchestral programme?"

"No, no. There won't be any music in it, Foster. Instead, I'd like you to go to Mutual Street Arena tonight and broadcast the hockey game between Parkdale and Kitchener Seniors."

"A what? A hockey game? Did I hear you right? Why wouldn't someone in the sports department do that job?"

"They haven't anyone with radio experience. No, you're our man, Foster. It could be that thirty, forty years from now you may be proud to say, 'I was the first person in all the world ever to broadcast a hockey game.'"

"That's quite a prophecy, Basil; but what if it's a flop?"

Foster Hewitt
1923

Although Canada had long held the right to negotiate international treaties, until the Halibut Fishery Treaty of 1923 Great Britain had always co-signed. But Prime Minister Mackenzie King insisted that the treaty, which set limits on halibut fishing in the Northern Pacific Ocean and the Bering Sea, was solely the concern of Canadians and Americans, and needed no British participation. When Britain acquiesced, the treaty became the first negotiated and signed solely by Canada, a precedent that advanced Canada well along the road to a completely independent foreign policy.

Duly ratified The nationals and inhabitants and the fishing vessels and boats, of the United States and of the Dominion of Canada, respectively, are hereby prohibited from fishing for halibut (Hippoglossus) both in the territorial waters and in the high seas off the western coasts of the United States, including Bering Sea, and of the Dominion of Canada, from the 16th day of November next after the date of the exchange of ratifications of this Convention, to the 15th day of the following February, both days inclusive, and within the same period yearly thereafter, provided that upon the recommendation of the International Fisheries Commission hereinafter described, this close season may be modified or suspended at any time after the expiration of three such seasons, by a special agreement concluded and duly ratified by the High Contracting Parties.

Halibut Fishery
Treaty
1923

Scottish-born James Bryton McLachlan immigrated to Cape Breton, Nova Scotia, where he became secretary-treasurer of District 26 of the United Mine Workers of America. McLachlan played an important role in the Cape Breton labour wars of the early 1920s, which lasted four years and accounted for millions of striker-days. This call to action, which was published in the *Maritime Labour Herald* in July 1923 and sent to miners' locals in District 26, came just before McLachlan's incarceration in Dorchester Penitentiary on charges of seditious libel.

Act at once **On Sunday evening last, these provincial police, in the most brutal manner, rode down the people of Whitney Pier, who were on the street...One woman, beaten over the head with a police club, gave premature birth to a child. The child is dead and the woman's life is despaired of...The government of Nova Scotia is the guilty and responsible party for this crime. No miner can remain at work while this government turns Sydney into a jungle: to do so, is to sink your manhood and allow Armstrong and his miserable bunch of grafting politicians to trample your last shred of freedom in the sand. Call a meeting of your local at once and decide to spread the fight against Armstrong to every mine in Nova Scotia. Act at once – tomorrow may be too late.**

James McLachlan
1923

James Shaver Woodsworth learned his socialist principles as a Methodist minister in a working-class district of Winnipeg before World War I and became one of the leading proponents of the Social Gospel, which preached the establishment of a Kingdom of God in the here and now. During the Winnipeg General Strike of 1919 he was charged with seditious libel for editorials he wrote in support of the strikers. In 1921, he was elected to the House of Commons as a member of the Labour Party. But judging by this excerpt from an article he wrote for *The Canadian Forum* in 1924, Canada's leading progressive of the 1920s would sound politically incorrect today.

Unassimilated blocks of Europeans **A number of factors contribute to render very difficult the formation and expression of new ideas and policies in Canada...**
    The heterogeneous character of our population prevents cultural unity. Exclude the French and the Jewish and other non-British groups and judged by the standards of Toronto, Montreal is about the size of Hamilton. In the West, there are large unassimilated blocks of Europeans who live in Canada in the flesh but spiritually live still in the old world. Ultimately these various cultures may blend into something new and higher. At present, they are almost mutually exclusive.

J.S. Woodsworth
1924

The following passage is from Mazo de la Roche's original novel about the Whiteoak family, a literary soap opera dominated by the central setting for which the novel is named, a house called Jalna. First published in 1927, *Jalna* won the $10,000 *Atlantic Monthly* award for the year's best novel and sold more than 100,000 copies in fewer than 12 months. De la Roche went on to write 15 sequels, the final one a year before she died, that between them have sold in excess of 9 million copies in their various editions.

Welcome 'ome **Eden looked down at her curiously. How would she and his family get on, he wondered. Now that he had brought her home he realized suddenly that she was alien to his family. He had a disconcerting sensation of surprise at finding himself married. After all, he was not so elated as he had expected to be when Rags opened the door and smiled a self-conscious welcome...**

Mazo de la Roche
1927

"Welcome 'ome, Mr Eden," he said, sadly. "Welcome 'ome, sir."

"Thanks, Rags. Alayne, this is Wragge, our – " Eden hesitated, trying to decide how Mr Wragge should be described, and continued, "our factotum."

"Welcome 'ome, Mrs Whiteoak," said Rags, with his curiously deprecating yet impudent glance. It said to Eden silently but unmistakably: "Ow, you may fool the family, young man, but you can't fool me. You 'aven't married a heiress. And 'ow we're to put up with another young woman 'ere, Gawd only knows."

Brevity and precision were Morley Callaghan's greatest literary assets. With encouragement from Ernest Hemingway, whom Callaghan met while working summers at the *Toronto Daily Star*, and F. Scott Fitzgerald, who recommended Callaghan to his publisher, Callaghan decided to become a writer. His first novel, *Strange Fugitive*, is the story of Harry Trotter, a lumberyard foreman who goes on to become a bootlegger and eventually dies at the hands of his rivals.

He felt almost like crying **He lay in bed one night, listening to Vera breathing and thinking he had loved her so much no other woman could ever give such satisfaction. He felt almost like crying, and wished he had encouraged her to have children. He was sure his increasing interest in other women had a direct relation to Vera, and that he would always be in love with her. It was a hot night and bed-clothes were tight against his throat or he might have dealt more success- fully with such a complicated problem. Then Vera moved beside him. She was awake. She began talking of an argument they had had before going to bed. She said sullenly that he thought more of his job than of anything else on earth. The thought startled him, and before falling asleep he decided she had been close to the truth.**

Morley Callaghan
1928

1939

Years of Despair "I remember those '30s sunrises, all dirty from the dust in the air, as I walked down to the town office early to get my paperwork done. No matter how early I went in, the men would be lined up, waiting, a long line in the street outside the office. Not much talk, nothing to say. Nowhere else to go, all the time in the world. Dust in their clothes, dust blowing around them.

"We opened the office at nine, and they would come in, one at a time, very orderly. There were farmers from the district, men I knew around town, people I'd known at school. And if they had ridden in on the rods from God knows where, they were the same kind of people. Decent Canadians who ought to be doing a job every day, not lining up for a dole we didn't have.

"I spent the days saying no to them. No, no work on offer. No, no food vouchers this week. No, no housing allotments. No, nothing we could do for their sick baby, nothing for the cattle they couldn't feed, nothing for the crop they couldn't sell, nothing to stop the bank foreclosing. That was life as a town manager in Saskatchewan in the 1930s. And the ones who knew me would say, 'Right, Cec. Thanks anyway.'"

In the Great Depression of the 1930s, you found yourself either in the half of the population that had a breadwinner or in the half of the population without one. And that made all the difference. You lived in a nation that grew and harvested and made things for the rest of the world. When the world could not buy, Canadians' work and income vanished. Governments seemed unable to launch any real attack on the crisis. Canadians threw out Prime Minister Mackenzie King for a Calgary lawyer, R.B. Bennett, and then threw Bennett out to bring King back. Ottawa fought with the provinces over the blame and the responsibility. Soup kitchens and relief camps gave no one hope.

"The town council cut my pay, but Mary and I were actually better off than we had been in the '20s. Anything we wanted, someone was selling off for a song, begging us to take it, trying to scrape together a few pennies to keep going. Big houses near us were on offer for next to nothing. Any time we wanted any little chore done, we had 50 people fighting over the chance to do it. But I got to hate my job.

"And we were the lucky ones. We had work. Those men in the lines, they had it so much worse. They always looked so beaten.

"I'm no radical. Those Reds and agitators in the work camps, they got what they deserved. But I could read in the papers about the Regina Manifesto those eggheads and Dr. Woodsworth from Winnipeg came up with. Getting governments to spend money, even if they had to borrow it. Getting the men working again and the money changing hands. It made a kind of sense to me, those mornings walking down to the town office to say no a thousand more times. We ought to be able to pull together, shouldn't we?

"I kept a mean, tough face on, all those years. I got pretty hard. I sent those men away with nothing, time after time, year after year. It wasn't my fault, but I did it.

"But what a pity it all seemed, what a waste. 'Right, Cec. Thanks anyway.'"

Visions 1930–1939

1930 May Construction workers atop the growing Confederation Life building on University Avenue in Toronto. A number of Canada's major buildings, begun when the economy was still booming, were completed in the early 1930s, even as jobs disappeared and the Depression deepened. In February 1930 Parliament had passed the Fair Wages and Eight Hour Day Act, which applied to public works or construction subsidized by government funds.

1930 June North America's first saints, the eight Jesuits killed by Iroquois in 1648 and 1649 – Jean de Brébeuf, Noel Chabanel, Antoine Daniel, Charles Garnier, René Goupil, Isaac Jogues, Jean de La Lande, and Gabriel Lalemant – were canonized. Monuments to the eight martyrs, including this one in Quebec, began springing up across the country. When Pope John Paul II visited Canada in 1984, the Martyrs' Shrine near Midland, Ontario, where the eight Jesuits lost their lives, was one of his places of pilgrimage.

1930 July Hard times fed prejudice, as evidenced by this Vancouver meeting of the
Ku Klux Klan. The late 1920s and early 1930s saw a brief flowering of the Klan across
Canada, primarily in Ontario and the West. With few blacks to target, the Canadian
Klan spat its venom at Jews, Asians, Catholics, and immigrants from southern Europe.
In February 1930, Klan members paraded boldly through Oakville, Ontario, lighting
a huge cross on the main street, in protest against an impending interracial marriage.

1930 August Hundreds of thousands of Canadians and Americans journeyed to the Saint-Hubert airfield near Montreal to gaze upon the giant British airship *R-100*, which had crossed the Atlantic in 77 hours and was making a triumphal Canadian visit to promote plans for an airship network that would link the mother country with the outposts of empire. The dirigible flew over Ottawa, Toronto, and Niagara Falls before returning to Montreal.

The *R-100*'s grand tour convinced many thousands of Canadians that regularly scheduled transatlantic airship travel was around the corner. They weren't alone. In the 1930s, before the airplane became a reliable long-distance carrier, airships looked to have the upper hand. But the fiery wreck of the *R-100*'s sister, the *R-101*, in October 1930 and then the crash of the *Hindenburg* in May 1937 punctured such notions.

1931 January Tobogganers enjoying a run past the majestic Château Frontenac Hotel in Quebec City (*left*). Despite hard times, Canadians still found ways to relax. By summer, the federal government had put $20 million into public works to provide jobs for those thrown out of work by the Depression. Soon almost half of all Canadians would have no income to depend upon; but low prices meant that even those earning an ordinary wage could live quite well. These vacationers at the Devil's Gap Camp and Lodge in Manitoba (*above*) could have stepped out of a much more prosperous decade.

1931 July At King William Island, William "Paddy" Gibson, chief trader of the Hudson's Bay Company in the Northwest Territories, examining the remains of members of Sir John Franklin's 1845 expedition in search of the Northwest Passage. Franklin's ships became trapped in the ice during the winter of 1845–46. Franklin died on June 11, 1847. The remainder of his crew perished the following winter.

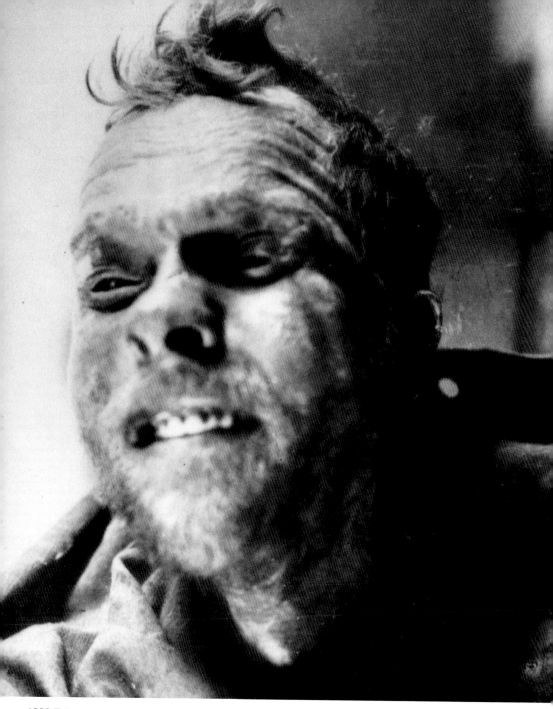

1932 February The most sensational news story of the new year was the seven-week pursuit through the Yukon and the Northwest Territories of Albert Johnson, whom the press referred to as "the Mad Trapper of Rat River." This photo of Johnson was taken after he was finally cornered and killed by an RCMP posse. He had shot one officer dead during an exchange of fire and wounded another while leading his trackers on a wild chase through the Subarctic winter.

1933 January By the start of the year, over 1.5 million Canadians were on some form of public relief and the official unemployment rate was 23 percent. Despite the Unemployment Relief Act of 1930, government help was inadequate for people evicted from their homes (*above*). In response to the rising tide of unemployment, the Department of National Defence organized relief camps for transient unemployed men. However, homelessness and poverty did not discriminate on the basis of gender or age.

Some symptoms of hard times (*top, far left to far right*): men playing cards in a relief camp bunkhouse in northern Ontario; Casa Loma, the faux-European château that bankrupted Sir Henry Pellatt, turned into a tourist attraction in Toronto; the worldly possessions of an evicted family in Montreal; a Saskatchewan homestead following a "black blizzard," or dust storm.

1933 April In Washington, D.C., Prime Minister R.B. Bennett shaking hands with President Franklin Roosevelt (*above*) at the opening of the World Economic Conference. In 1935, Bennett surprised many observers by embracing much of Roosevelt's interventionist program and attempting to Canadianize it with the "Bennett New Deal." But public opinion had already turned against him. Those who could not afford gasoline referred to their livestock-drawn vehicles as "Bennett Buggies" (*top right*) – in bitter contrast to the limo transporting the wealthy bachelor PM and his sister (*lower right*).

1933 May The Canadian Radio Broadcasting Commission, precursor of the CBC, began broadcasting from Montreal in both English and French (*top left*, a 1930s radio drama). Canadians found different ways of tuning out the hard times, including eight-day marathon cycling races such as the one advertised here (*top right*). The moving pictures were booming, among them several films featuring a Canadian Indian named Grey Owl (*above*), who was really an Englishman named Archie Belaney. Meanwhile, "Canadian Dance Sensation" Colette and Barry (*right*) wowed the ballroom-dance crowd.

1933 June Political activists had plenty to protest, between the plight of workers and the disturbing growth of fascism and anti-Semitism both in Europe and across Canada. The anti-fascist cause was taken up by groups such as the Young Communist League. *Top:* Members of Toronto's Jewish community, many of whom had recently immigrated to Canada, marching against anti-Semitism. On the labour front, the railway town of Stratford saw a bitter general strike that fall (*above*).

1934 December Tim Buck addressing a mass rally at Maple Leaf Gardens (*above*) following his release from prison. As the Depression worsened, the Communist Party's ranks swelled, and those in power reacted by infiltrating its ranks and arresting its leaders. The most famous arrests had occurred on August 11, 1931, when police charged Buck, its general secretary, and seven others with sedition and membership in an illegal organization.

1934 May Although a lingerie advertisement in the Better Living Building at the 1934 Canadian National Exhibition would proclaim girdles to be the sensation of the decade, the unforgettable highlight of the year and the decade was the birth of five tiny girls to the impoverished Dionne family of Corbeil, Ontario, who already had five children. As the first surviving quintuplets in the history of the human species, the babies (*opposite, top*, with their mother, Elzire) became instant international stars.

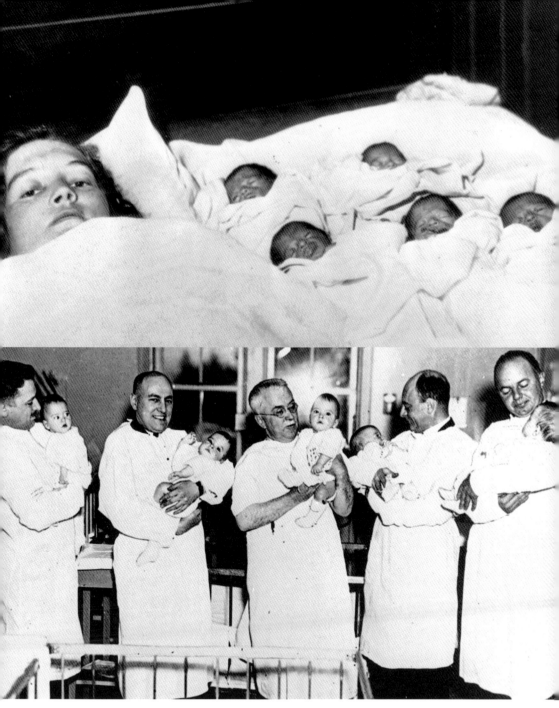

It wasn't long before the Ontario government took custody of the five girls for profit, political and financial. Dr. Allan Roy Dafoe (*above*, middle), who delivered the quints and became their guardian, found himself hobnobbing with celebrities that included the four Ontario cabinet ministers pictured here. (Premier Mitch Hepburn is at the far right.) Millions of visitors came from around the world to visit the Dionne Quintuplets in Quintland, their government-built nursery in Callander, Ontario.

1935 June Young women participating in Farm Girls Week at the University of Saskatchewan at Saskatoon benefitted from "a course in community leadership embracing domestic and leisure time activities," including how to make preserves. Few feminine faces can be found in the graduation pictures from Canadian universities, where female enrolment had peaked at 23.5 percent of all undergraduates in 1930.

Women were most visible in programs such as nursing and domestic science, which trained them to keep the traditional woman's place. But a few remarkable women did prevail against the norm. Agnes Macphail, one of only two female voices in Parliament (her colleague was Martha Black, elected from the Yukon), fought a lonely battle for prison reform. "No man has the right," she told the House, "to deprive another of space, and light, and air!"

1935 June Unemployed men living in West Coast relief camps changing trains during their "On to Ottawa" trek to demand a guaranteed minimum wage. By the time the trekkers, who set out from Kamloops, British Columbia, reached Regina, they numbered 2,000. But on July 1, in what became known as the Dominion Day Riot, the authorities moved in to arrest the trek leaders and a police detective was killed. Public support evaporated and the protest disbanded. Ironically, unemployment began to decline soon afterwards and wheat harvests revived. The worst of the Depression would soon be over.

1935 August The Social Credit Party won the Alberta provincial election. During the campaign, a radio evangelist turned politician, William Aberhart (*top*), persuaded Albertans that he had a simple solution to the Depression: give people money so they would have more buying power. His posters could be found everywhere, including the backs of railroad flatcars (*above*). Although the Social Credit Party trounced the reigning United Farmers of Alberta, Aberhart soon downplayed Social Credit doctrine in favour of the more traditionally conservative policies that would keep his party in power until 1971.

1936 April Mrs. D.E. Robertson (*top*) listening over headphones to her husband, one of three men buried alive in a gold mine collapse at Moose River, Nova Scotia, that transfixed the continent for 10 days. Meanwhile Michael Dwyer, Nova Scotia minister of mines (*above*, middle), directed the rescue operation. J. Frank Willis of the fledgling Canadian Radio Broadcasting Commission broadcast an unprecedented 69 hours of non-stop coverage that was carried throughout the U.S. and Canada. On April 23, newpapers ran headlines of the rescue of two of the three trapped miners (*right*), one of them Robertson.

1936 July At Arras, France, 19 years after Canada's greatest victory of World War I, veterans, their wives, and widows of those who fell gathered (*left*) for the unveiling by King Edward VIII of the Vimy Ridge Memorial (*above*), designed by Walter Allward. The memorial, which stands 27 metres high, is part of a 100-hectare park dedicated to the 3,598 Canadians who died taking Vimy Ridge in April 1917. Only four years after the unveiling, another war would be on, and the German army would reoccupy Vimy.

1936 November Members of an Edmonton vaudeville troop rehearsing a dance number in costumes that look uncannily like parodies of prison camp attire. While vaudeville distracted many Canadians from the world's troubles, the rise of fascism galvanized many others into action, especially Dr. Norman Bethune, a brilliant Montreal surgeon who was also a dedicated Communist. Bethune went to Spain to serve as a medical officer for the Republican forces in the Spanish Civil War.

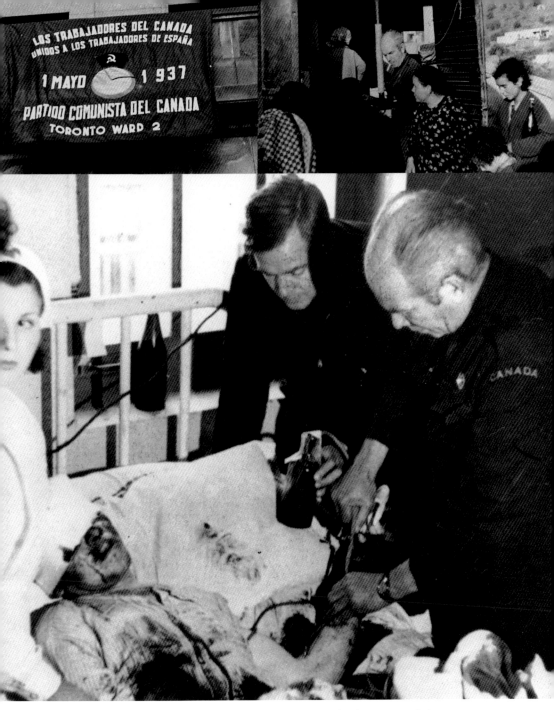

1937 May More than 1,200 Canadians followed Bethune to Spain as part of the Mackenzie-Papineau Battalion, which joined the Republican fight against General Franco even though the King government outlawed their participation. In Barcelona, a May Day banner (*top left*) celebrated the solidarity of Canadian and Spanish workers during the war. Bethune was everywhere, helping refugees onto his first aid truck (*top right*) or operating on war casualties (*above*, assisted by Henning Sorenson). He revolutionized war medicine by performing the first battlefield blood transfusions.

1937 June Prime Minister Mackenzie King visiting Berlin, Germany. King complimented Adolf Hitler on his success in rebuilding the country. At the conclusion of his talks with the Führer and other German leaders, King announced that he had succeeded in promoting "understanding, friendship and goodwill."

After the trip King wrote in his diary: "[Hitler's] face is much more prepossessing than his pictures would give the impression of. It is not that of a fiery, over-strained nature, but of a calm, passive man, deeply and thoughtfully in earnest. His skin was smooth; his face did not present lines of fatigue or weariness; his eyes impressed me most of all. There was a liquid quality about them which indicate keen perception and profound sympathy."

1938 June Police arresting members of the Relief Project Worker's Union outside the Vancouver Post Office, which they had occupied, along with the Vancouver Art Gallery, for several weeks in a sit-down strike. On June 19, nicknamed Bloody Sunday, Mounties and city police used tear gas to evict the strikers. A number of the strikers were wounded in the ensuing skirmish, including this bleeding combatant (*right*).

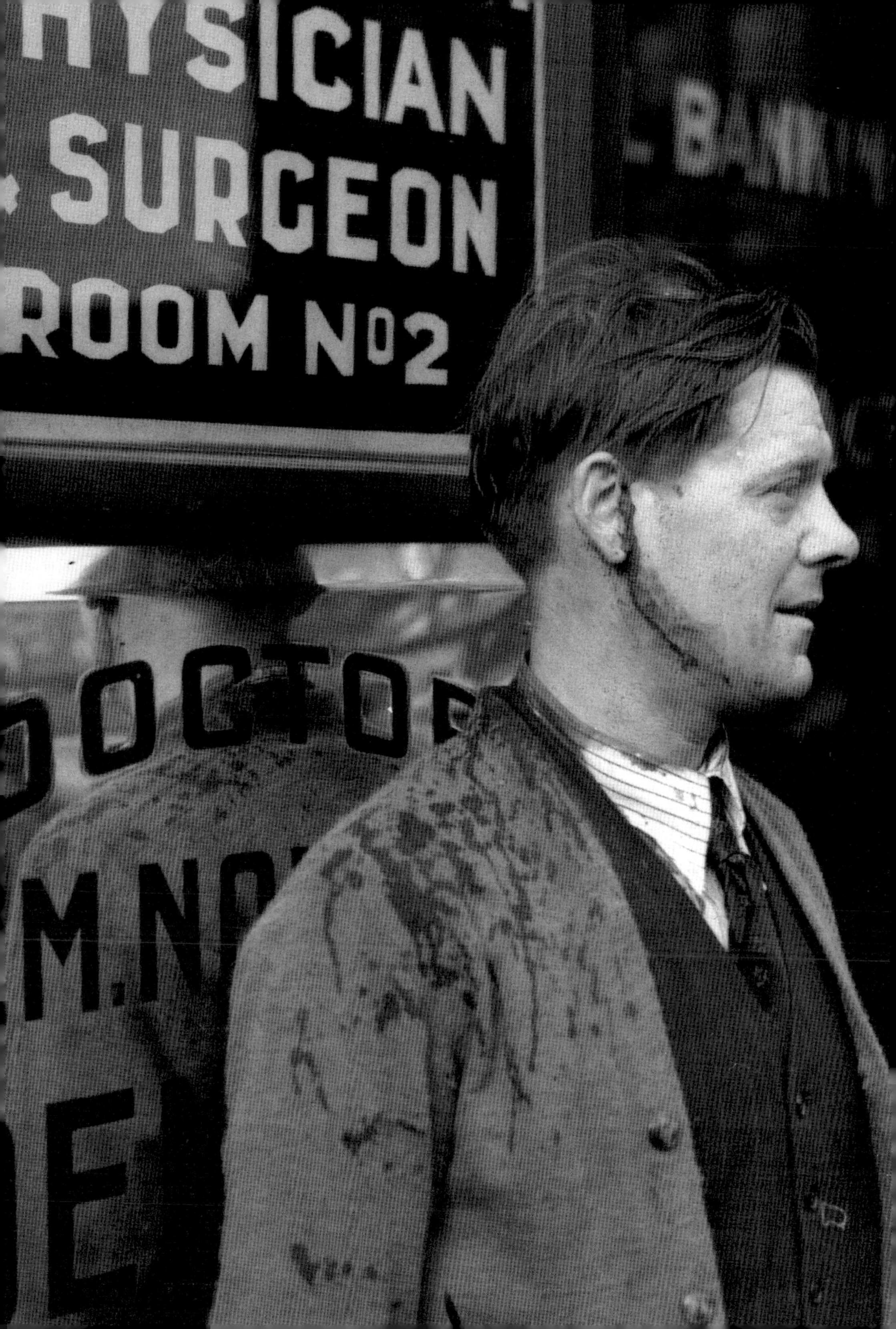
HYSICIAN
SURGEON
ROOM No2

1939 May King George VI and Queen Elizabeth (later the Queen Mother) arrived in Canada for a state visit, an event that gave great pleasure to Depression-weary citizens. Among the highlights of the royal progress, during which the couple crossed Canada twice, were the unveiling of the National War Memorial in Ottawa and the laying of the cornerstone of the Supreme Court of Canada. Countless mementos of the King and Queen's visit filled windows like this one in Vancouver's Chinatown.

1939 June Before heading home, the King and Queen opened the Canada Pavilion at
the World's Fair in New York. The architecture of the fair was characterized by modernist
monuments whose long curvilinear and streamlined forms reflected the collective desire
of a generation, still suffering from a crisis of confidence in the wake of the Depression,
to embrace an industrial democratic future. Modernism celebrated the age of technology
and the promise that a better tomorrow was within everyone's grasp.

1939 June An anti-Semitic sign in Sainte-Agathe, Quebec, typifying the strong anti-Jewish sentiment throughout Canada on the eve of World War II. During June, the 907 Jewish refugees aboard the Hamburg-American liner *St. Louis*, later immortalized in the movie *The Voyage of the Damned*, were refused entry into Canada, their last hope of refuge. In the House of Commons Justice Minister Ernest Lapointe spoke for many when he "emphatically opposed" allowing the ship to land. Among Western nations, Canada took fewer Jewish refugees as a percentage of its population than any other.

1939 June At a mass marriage ceremony in Montreal, 105 young Catholic couples on their way to exchanging holy vows. Group weddings seem to have been an effort by the church to bolster its hold on the young as the war loomed. (Canada declared war on Germany on September 10.) Officially the Quebec church would support the war effort, but at the parish level there was frequent dissent from the party line. Some priests even refused to read announcements about Victory Bonds from their pulpits.

Voices 1930–1939

Radio was one of the few affordable sources of entertainment during the Dirty Thirties. Home-grown radio drama premiered with the *Romance of Canada* series in 1931 and the Canadian Broadcasting Corporation was established in 1936. But the earliest radio memory for many Canadians, including R.H. Hahn (who shared this story with the authors of *Signing On: The Birth of Radio in Canada*), was American.

Sitting around the crystal sets
Around 1930, when I was seven or eight, I remember people sitting around with crystal sets at our homestead in northern Saskatchewan listening to the World Series. Only one person at a time could hear the thing. They'd share this little ear plug. I was never important enough to get a turn. There'd be a group of maybe twenty grown men at these gatherings, each taking a brief moment to hear what was going on and then reporting it to everyone else.

R.H. Hahn
1930

Harold Adams Innis's experiences as a front-line soldier during World War I led him to study the way colonies like Canada develop. With his first book, *The Fur Trade in Canada*, from which the following passage is taken, Innis laid the foundation for his ground-breaking studies of communications theory, which profoundly influenced Marshall McLuhan.

The center and the margin
The economic history of Canada has been dominated by the discrepancy between the center and the margin of western civilization. Energy has been directed toward the exploitation of staple products and the tendency has been cumulative. The raw material supplied to the mother country stimulated manufactures of the finished product and also of the products which were in demand in the colony. Large-scale production of raw materials was encouraged by improvement of technique of production, of marketing, and of transport as well as by improvement in the manufacture of the finished product. As a consequence, energy in the colony was drawn into the production of the staple commodity both directly and indirectly. Population was involved directly in the production of the staple and indirectly in the production of facilities promoting production. Agriculture, industry, transportation, trade, finance, and governmental activities tend to become subordinate to the production of the staple for a more highly specialized manufacturing community. These general tendencies may be strengthened by governmental policy as in the mercantile system but the importance of these policies varies in particular industries. Canada remained British in spite of free trade and chiefly because she continued as an exporter of staples to a progressively industrialized mother country.

Harold Innis
1930

Although Emily Carr is best known for her painting, her first book, *Klee Wyck*, won a Governor General's Award. On March 4, 1930, Carr had this to say on the occasion of her first exhibition in her home town, Victoria, British Columbia.

The camera has no mind The camera cannot comment. The camera cannot select. The camera cannot feel, it is purely mechanical.

*Emily Carr
1930*

By the aid of our own reinforcement we can perceive roughly what we desire to perceive and ignore, as far as is physically possible, what we do not desire to perceive. No work of real value is produced by an artist unless his hand obeys his mind. The camera has no mind.

We may copy some thing as faithfully as the camera, but unless we bring to our picture something additional – something creative – something of ourselves – our picture does not live.

Like many intellectuals in the 1930s, Dorothy Livesay was attracted to Communism as a solution to the social and economic disaster through which she was living. Although now remembered as a sensitive poet with a remarkable range, Livesay was also a lifelong political activist and champion of women's rights. The following passage is from *Right Hand Left Hand*, a collection of essays, poems, letters, and reminiscences of her involvement in the Communist Party.

Brutality and fear The culmination of this first stage of struggle took place in March, 1933, when an unemployed worker, Nick Zynchuk, entered a house where an eviction was taking place, to obtain his few belongings. He was shot in the back, killed outright, by a policeman. The storm of protest at this action brought 20,000 workers to his funeral. Then the police attacked, on horseback and on foot, tearing down the banners, slugging men, women and children, following wounded workers to the hospital to arrest them. As a follow-up of this brutality, fear halted the progressive movement. The "Canadian Labor Defense League," as well as the underground "Communist Party," were too weak to go forward. Reaction set in. For a year it was impossible to hold demonstrations of more than a handful of unemployed; and always the police attacked viciously. This was the year in which fascist organizations, appealing to the veterans, the unemployed and the small traders, advanced by leaps and bounds.

*Dorothy Livesay
1934*

William Aberhart was an apolitical Baptist minister and high school principal until 1932, when he embraced a new economic theory known as Social Credit. Motivated by the terrible dilemma of "poverty in the midst of plenty," Aberhart began to use his Sunday-afternoon radio show to preach the Social Credit doctrine. Although never able to fulfill his new creed's promise after becoming premier of Alberta in 1935, he managed to remain in office until his death in 1943. In 1934 he laid out his vision before members of the Alberta legislature.

Social Credit

Social Credit I am fully conscious of the responsibility that falls upon me in making an appeal for the introduction of a system of credit to solve the present depression...I am equally aware of the responsibility that rests upon the members of this Government in passing judgment on this matter. If the task of the juryman gives him concern when one man's life or property hangs in the balance, what must be the case when the lives, the prosperity, and the happiness of 700,000 people await your judgment...

Let us remember that our province is potentially a land of plenty. None of our citizens should be suffering from want or privation. The granaries are full and goods are piled high in the storehouses. We have an abundance of foodstuffs that are being wasted, or wantonly destroyed. Why then should many of our people be in dire need, in suffering from worry, from privation, and from hopelessness?

*William Aberhart
1934*

Francis Reginald Scott made equally important contributions to law, literature, and politics. As a poet he was a leading voice of modernism. As an engaged citizen, he helped found the League for Social Reconstruction, which hatched many of the tenets of the soon-to-be-founded Co-operative Commonwealth Federation. But as his satire of a meeting of the Canadian Authors Association indicates, he also had a good sense of humour.

The Canadian Authors Meet

...The cakes are sweet, but sweeter is the feeling
That one is mixing with the literati;
It warms the old, and melts the most congealing.
Really, it is a most delightful party.

Shall we go round the mulberry bush, or shall
We gather at the river, or shall we
Appoint a Poet Laureate this fall,
Or shall we have another cup of tea?

O Canada, O Canada, Oh can
A day go by without new authors springing
To paint the native maple, and to plan
More ways to set the selfsame welkin ringing?

*F.R. Scott
1935*

Richard Bedford Bennett gained office in 1930 by promising aggressive measures to combat the deepening economic crisis. Instead the Depression deepened and his popularity plummeted. Early in 1935 he abandoned his conservative businesslike approach to government, announcing a "new deal" based on the reforms of U.S. President Roosevelt during a dramatic series of radio broadcasts. The "Bennett New Deal" called for a guaranteed minimum wage, health and unemployment insurance, and government regulation of banking and trade. Voters weren't convinced, however, and brought back Mackenzie King in the 1935 election.

Equality in economic conditions Labour in one part of Canada must not be at a disadvantage with labour in another part. That is wrong socially and it is foolish in a business sense, for clearly it creates a disequilibrium in the nation's industrial life. There must be an end to child labour. There must be an end to sweat shop conditions. There must be an end to the reckless exploitation of human resources and the trafficking in the health and happiness of Canadian citizens. There must be an end to the idea that a workman should be held to his labour throughout the daylight hours of every day. I for one, believe that our workers must have more leisure.

*R.B. Bennett
1935*

Worst hit by the Great Depression was the prairie wheat belt, where years of adequate rainfall had disguised the unsuitability of much land for grain growing. Overuse had caused fertile topsoil to blow away and the long drought of the 1930s ruined many prairie farmers. The following reminiscence from *Ten Lost Years* by Barry Broadfoot vividly evokes the hard times in the Canadian West.

The terrible winters The 'hoppers. People at the door begging, for a sandwich, a meal, a cement patch for their tire, a glass of water, the school teacher who boarded with us crying because the board couldn't pay her any more and were closing down the school and she had to go away and she was in love with a local lad...The terrible winters. People getting caught on the roads and some freezing to death. Yes, that happened. Good friends leaving for the coast, and then writing back and asking how things were, were they getting any better, was there any point in coming back home again?

*Anonymous
circa 1936*

In 1936, Montreal surgeon Henry Norman Bethune organized the world's first mobile blood transfusion unit while volunteering as a Republican army surgeon during the Spanish Civil War. Handsome and articulate, Bethune was equally skilled with the scalpel and with the pen. Witness his description of the bombing of the port town of Almeria.

A bright flame of hate

Norman Bethune
1936

The siren alarms sounded thirty seconds before the first bomb fell. These planes made no effort to hit the government battleship in the harbour or bomb the barracks. They deliberately dropped ten great bombs in the very center of the town where on the main street were sleeping huddled together on the pavement so closely that a car could pass only with difficulty, the exhausted refugees. After the planes had passed I picked up in my arms three dead children from the pavement in front of the Provincial Committee for the Evacuation of Refugees where they had been standing in a great queue waiting for a cupful of preserved milk and a handful of dried bread, the only food some of them had for days. The street was a shambles of the dead and dying, lit only by the orange glare of burning buildings. In the darkness the moans of the wounded children, shrieks of agonized mothers, the curses of the men rose in a massed cry higher and higher to a pitch of intolerable intensity. One's body felt as heavy as the dead themselves, but empty and hollow, and in one's brain burned a bright flame of hate.

No Canadian politician has exhibited more skill than Mackenzie King at sitting on the fence – or at staying in office, which was where he sat when Hitler invaded Poland in September 1939. Here Prime Minister King addresses the House of Commons as he assumes the responsibility of leading Canada into World War II.

Nothing but chaos

William Lyon
Mackenzie King
1939

Hitler has said: "Whoever lights the torch of war in Europe can wish for nothing but chaos." "Nothing but chaos"; that is what the leader of the Nazi party in Germany is seeking to bring upon the world to-day. And it is to prevent chaos becoming the fate of this and other lands that it becomes our duty, as citizens of Canada, to stand to a man in the defence of our country and at the side of Great Britain in the defence of freedom.

1949

Battle and Beyond "I was just a big strong kid, working on the seine boats out of Steveston after the Japanese got rounded up. I took care of myself, I didn't really give a damn about the war. But I figured if I didn't join, there was going to be conscription anyway. After I signed up in '43, I happened to see the old man outside a bootlegger down on Hastings. Probably that's what I was getting away from.

"They sent me over to England as a rifleman in a re-placement unit for Third Canadian Division. We went across to Normandy right after the big landing, when the generals were pouring us into the bridgehead by divisions.

"You knew there was a war on. Trucks and Jeeps and armour grinding up from the beaches, and regiments get-ting themselves sorted out. All the buildings smashed, and burned-out tanks and guns, and dead cows stinking up the whole countryside. Artillery pounding all the time, fighter-bombers going in. And everyone going full tilt, because the war was just up the hill, ready and waiting.

"The Third Division had got hit hard pretty on the beaches. I was sent to the North Shore Regiment, which really got clobbered at a place called Carpiquet outside Caen. They had hardly been in action three weeks, and they had a lot of room for replacements! A rifleman's life expectancy was pretty close to nothing.

"You get to know an army when you are going to die in it. Pretty soon I wasn't counting on living very long, but I'd found something I belonged to. The North Shore Regiment was Scotch and French guys, mostly, from up Miramichi way in New Brunswick. I'd never even been in New Brunswick, but soon I loved the North Shore like I'd spent my life there. The North Shore Regiment meant more to me than my family ever had.

"Normandy, that was rough. The Scheldt was worse. That was October, wet, cold. Those canals and channels were hell to get across, and as soon as you got a handful of guys over, the Germans would counterattack to push you back in. By then I was one of the veterans.

"I got on this burial detail one night, and the padre told me he had buried more men here than in his whole life at home. He was a serious young Presbyterian from Nova Scotia, and pretty close to cracking. Killed later on, or so I heard.

"Later, when they pulled us out of the line for a bit, they brought in one of those entertainment units. A troupe sang that song, big hit at home, 'And when you get back, and you will get back, you'll find the whole world waiting for you!'

"You know what I did? I walked out of the tent and I upchucked on the ground outside. See, I'd got used to the idea that I wasn't going home. Then these singers and dancers and comedians came along, and it struck me, some of the fellows did have the world waiting: civvy street and girls to meet. Suddenly I was not so sure why I was all set to buy the farm, and it took me a few days before I found my stomach for more fighting. I still get queasy every time I hear Wayne and Shuster. Funny fellows, but they take me right back to the war.

"But you can't talk like that now. How do you explain when you were so caught up in a war that the idea you might live through it made you sick to your stomach?"

Visions 1940–1949

1940 June Private Jack Bernard of the Duke of Connaught's Own Rifles bidding goodbye to his five-year-old son, Warren, in New Westminster, British Columbia. By the time Private Bernard had crossed the Atlantic, Paris had fallen. The First Canadian Infantry Brigade, after landing briefly in Brittany, had joined the ignominious withdrawal from the continent. Many who had fought in the 1914–18 war watched their sons march off in 1939 and 1940. But Canadians, especially the legions of unemployed, enlisted in droves – even in Quebec. For once, the country seemed to be united.

1941 December In a speech to Parliament, British Prime Minister Winston Churchill – caught here in the iconic Karsh photograph taken during his visit to Ottawa – exhorted Canadians to support the war effort. But he brought down the House when he commented sarcastically on the prediction that Hitler would wring England's neck like a chicken. After a magnificent pause, the great man intoned, "Some chicken! Some neck!" Canadian women supported the war effort in many ways, including taking on previously male jobs and performing in Victory Shows (*above*, a glimpse backstage in Nova Scotia).

1941 April A Montreal shopkeeper displaying a rationing sign. As shortages grew, rationing spread to items ranging from meat and butter to oil and gas, but prices remained stable, thanks to the Wartime Prices and Trade Board, which established an effective regime of wage and price controls. Minister of Munitions and Supply C.D. Howe pumped up the Canadian economy with tax concessions, cheap loans to business, and $1.5 billion in direct investment. New jobs plus military enlistment soon banished unemployment.

1941 May Young and old alike had been mobilized to produce a whole panoply of munitions and equipment, including 815,729 transport vehicles and 1,767,392 small arms in less than two years. In May, the first Canadian-made tank rolled off an assembly line in Montreal. Mackenzie King seized the war as an opportunity to revitalize the Canadian economy: "We are the bridge between the old world and the new; the bridge which joins the new freedom of the North American continent with the ancient freedom of Britain."

1942 February Two Japanese fishermen in Vancouver being questioned by an officer of the Royal Canadian Navy. After Japan bombed the U.S. naval base at Pearl Harbor, Canada joined Britain and the United States in declaring war on Japan. Within days the authorities began rounding up Canadians of Japanese origin. Japanese living in the coastal regions of British Columbia were removed to the interior and their property was confiscated. Japanese Canadians, many of them citizens, were shipped in cattle trucks to work camps or to prairie farms, where they spent the duration of the war.

228

1942 June Students at St. Mary's School in North Vancouver rehearsing for a possible Japanese attack by donning gas masks during class. Many Canadians and Americans expected an attack at any minute. On June 20, a Japanese U-boat fired a few shells at Estevan Point on Vancouver Island, which was the closest the war ever came to the Canadian West Coast – unless you count the thousands of American servicemen who flooded Alberta, British Columbia, and the Yukon to build the Alaska Highway, meant to transport troops north if the Japanese struck.

1943 January Mail order clerks in the Eaton's catalogue department. During World War II women entered the Canadian workforce in unprecedented numbers, once again taking up many traditionally male jobs – but once again at wages lower than men earned. Governments encouraged married women to get jobs by offering tax concessions and free nurseries. Such inducements disappeared once the war was over.

1943 February Members of the Canadian Women's Army Corps (CWAC) enjoying
a cigarette after taking part in a firefighting demonstration in London, England.
All three armed services recruited women in World War II, and a total of more than
45,000 signed on. Most performed clerical or other traditional "women's" work at
pay two-thirds that of a man with equivalent rank, but a number took on technical trades.
The women's services were disbanded after the war.

1943 June Ottawa's elite attended the christening of Princess Margriet of the Netherlands, whose family spent the war in Canada. The Dutch royals lived at Stornoway, later the residence of the leader of the opposition. In thanks for Canada's hospitality, Crown Princess Juliana presented the continuing annual gift of thousands of tulips that now bloom each spring around Ottawa. Canadian-Dutch friendship was further strengthened when Canadian troops led the liberation of Holland in 1944.

1943 December Soldiers from the First Canadian Division captured the Adriatic port town of Ortona, Italy, after a costly battle that involved a house-to-house advance through the town. Matthew Halton, reporting for CBC Radio, described the fighting thus: "The Germans were demons; the Canadians were possessed by demons. The more murderous the battle, the harder both sides fought…" According to the Canadian commander, Major General Christopher Vokes, "Everything before Ortona was a nursery tale."

1944 January Johnny Wayne and Frank Shuster performing a skit in *The Army Show.*
The two young comics, who met at Toronto's Harbord Collegiate, had just broken into radio
when they decided to enlist in 1941. After the war they became Canadian comedic icons.

1944 April Referee King Clancy, formerly a star with the Toronto Maple Leafs, assisting
a bleeding Jimmy Orlando of the Detroit Red Wings, following a fight with Gaye Stewart
of the Leafs during the Stanley Cup playoffs.

1944 January As the Allies advanced from Sicily to the Italian mainland, the First
Canadian Division moved up the Adriatic coast. Images of the Italian campaign (*clockwise
from top left*): near Ortona, a medical truck entering a town nicknamed Vancouver
by Canadian troops; members of the Saskatchewan Light Infantry taking an outdoor
shower; a desk officer trying to keep his mind off pin-ups and on logistics; soldiers in
the Royal Canadian Artillery shelling Sicilian positions near Missoria. *Right:* A picture
of the Führer was placed in the hand of a dead German during the Battle of Ortona.

1944 June Members of the Ninth Canadian Infantry Brigade wading ashore at Bernières sur Mer during the D-Day landings. Among the 9,000 Allied casualties were 1,074 Canadians (359 killed). But the campaign for northwest Europe had only begun, and the Canadians would be engaged continuously until May 1945.

German prisoners captured during the Normandy invasion carrying a stretcher bearing a wounded Canadian soldier (*above*). Many German POWs spent the rest of the war in Canada, some of them living in internment camps while working in the forest industry. Quite a few were so taken with the country that they returned as immigrants after the war.

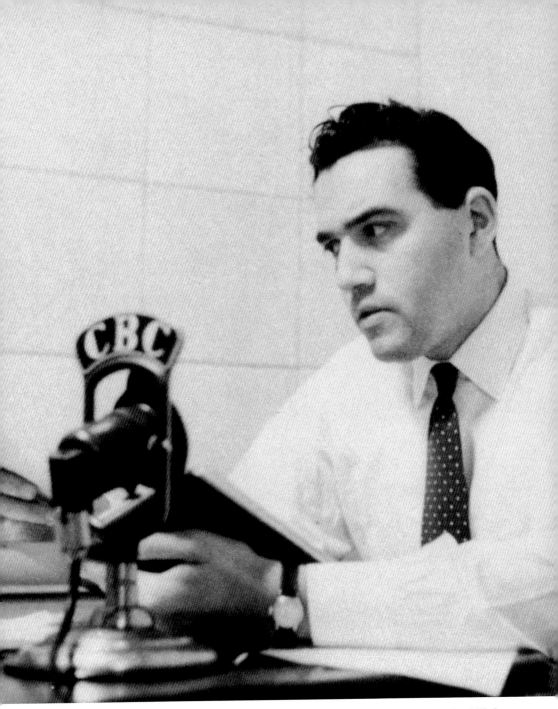

1944 September The First Canadian Army took Falaise, closing a gap in the Allied advance and trapping 50,000 German soldiers in the final stages of the battle for Normandy. The news was probably broadcast by Lorne Greene, "the Voice of Doom," the first announcer for the CBC when it introduced its own national news service in 1941. In Italy, First Canadian Corps broke through the German Gothic Line and helped liberate the Po Valley.

Also on the home front: C.D. Howe, minister of munitions and supply, was called the wizard of Canada's massive war industry. A munitions worker presented him with the ceremonial 100,000th shell (*above*). On the streets of Regina (*top left*) – and across Canada – bond drives were held throughout the war. Canada's air force (*top right*, a formation of Spitfires) grew rapidly in World War II thanks to the British Commonwealth Air Training Plan, which trained over 130,000 men on Canadian soil, more than half of them Canadian.

1944 October Pauline Vanier, wife of Georges Vanier, Canada's ambassador to France, laying a wreath at the Tomb of the Unknown Soldier at Dieppe, where Canada had suffered one of its worst defeats in the raid of August 1942. More than 900 of the 5,000 Canadian troops died and nearly 2,000 were taken prisoner.

Georges Vanier became the first French-Canadian governor general in 1959, and Madame Vanier was a beloved figure during her husband's eight-year tenure. She was admired for her exceptional service to humanity: she served as the first female chancellor of the University of Ottawa, founded the Vanier Institute for the Family, and supported numerous social welfare institutions.

1945 May Sailors walking down a Halifax street with looted liquor after Prime Minister Mackenzie King and his Quebec lieutenant, Louis St. Laurent, broadcast the news of victory in Europe. What began as a disorganized celebration in the port city, home base to thousands of naval personnel, turned into an ugly rampage after crowds became intoxicated. Two people died and many shops were destroyed.

Jubilant Dutch civilians celebrating their liberation from German occupation by the Canadian army. By the final year of the war, Canada's commitment to the conflict had grown enormously. There were almost a million men in arms in the three services. Our navy was the world's third largest, our air force ranked fourth. In the end, all three services suffered heavily, but the air force lost the most – 17,101 men, including 10,000 in the costly and controversial bomber offensive.

1946 March War brides and their children arriving in Halifax from overseas, having been granted free passage by the Canadian government. The immigration of more than 47,000 war brides along with nearly 22,000 children created an unusual social problem. Even though the majority came from Great Britain, many of the women had difficulty adjusting to their new country, including the harsh Canadian winters. The government issued each bride with a Canadian cookbook. After that, they were on their own.

The end of the war also meant the end of rationing, a move generally celebrated, as this flag-bedecked gas station in Toronto suggests. In November 1946, Mackenzie King announced the end of wartime wage and price controls, to the delight of organized labour and the anxiety of large employers, who foresaw union demands for big raises. And in Ontario, drinkers could rejoice in Premier George Drew's December announcement that after a 30-year prohibition it would once again be legal to purchase liquor by the glass.

1946 August Premier Maurice Duplessis (with scroll) standing beside Montreal Archbishop Joseph Charbonneau at the opening of the Sainte-Thérèse Bridge near Montreal. Given Duplessis's brand of Quebec nationalism – conservative, Catholic, and inward-looking – the two men should have been natural allies. But the Union Nationale premier had already begun dismantling the power of the church over Quebec society. Less than three years later, Duplessis and Charbonneau would find themselves in a very public battle for the allegiance of Quebec workers.

1946 Spring After being signed by Branch Rickey, president and general manager of the Brooklyn Dodgers, Jackie Robinson arrived in Montreal to play for the Dodgers' farm team, paving the way for his promotion to the big leagues and his breaking of the colour bar in professional sports. En route to Montreal he was bumped from an airplane so that a white passenger could have his seat. Robinson, here sliding into home plate, was known as "the Dark Destroyer" and went on to achieve one of the most glorious careers in baseball history.

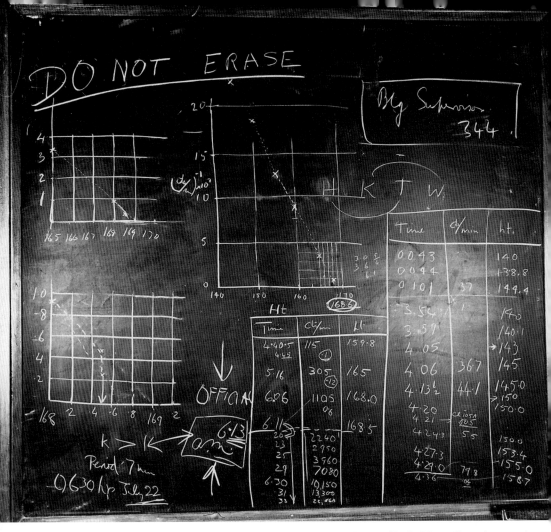

1947 June A blackboard at Canada's atomic research station at Chalk River, Ontario, sitting unattended as the NRX reactor went into operation. This 10-megawatt reactor seeded research that led to the CANDU power-generating reactor.

1947 September Former servicemen and servicewomen attending a physics lecture at the University of British Columbia in Vancouver. Canadians who had been in the services received Re-establishment Credits to defray the cost of postwar education.

1947 Autumn A publicity shot for Canadian Pacific Airlines shows off a DC-3, workhorse of its fleet. Canadian Pacific Railway had acquired several small airlines, mostly in the West, to form its airline during the war. CP Air's transcontinental ambitions weren't realized until 1958, when it was given permission to run a single daily service.

1948 February World champion skater Barbara Ann Scott (*right*) dazzled the world at the 1948 Winter Olympics at San Moritz, Switzerland, where she won gold.

Öffnungsfeier / Opening of the Olympic Games

...ton, den 2... ...ar 1948

Ein farbenfrohes Bild
...ten die Fahnen der a...
...ven Nationen / The fl...
of the competing natio...
added a gay pictur...

...ritz, der...
...Olympic G...es
...men Photo-Jeck und R...

...ey International
...en aller Wettkä...
...rmel / Bibi To...
...ternational to...
...r of all compe...

1948 Summer A john eyeing two prostitutes in a staged documentation of Montreal's red light district. In the postwar years Montreal was still the largest and most cosmopolitan city in Canada, with a reputation for both high life and low life. In a province dominated by Catholic morality, sexual adventuring was officially anathema. In practice, however, a john had little to fear. Police rarely bothered houses of ill repute, and when streetwalkers found themselves before a judge they were usually charged with loitering.

1949 February An illegal strike by 5,000 members of the Canadian Catholic Confederation of Labour began at Asbestos, Quebec, and spread to other mines, paralyzing Quebec's asbestos industry and polarizing its society for four months. On one side was the government of Maurice Duplessis, who branded the strikers saboteurs and sent in the police. On the other was a phalanx of progressive Catholics and intellectuals, including union leader Jean Marchand, 29-year-old activist Pierre Trudeau, and Archbishop Joseph Charbonneau, who denounced the government's actions as "a conspiracy against the working class."

255

1949 April At the Parliament Buildings, Prime Minister Louis St. Laurent, who had inherited the Liberal leadership from King in 1948, carved the first notches in a blank shield that would become the coat of arms of Canada's tenth province. Newfoundland formally joined Canada on March 31, after narrowly voting for union in a referendum. A fiery broadcaster named Joey Smallwood, who had led the pro-Canada forces, became the province's first premier. (He would win the May election for the Liberals in a landslide.) *Right:* A proud father in St. John's bathing his son, now a Canadian citizen.

1949 June Residents of Chicoutimi, Quebec, turned their gaze away from the war-torn 1940s and towards the unknown 1950s. The economy was humming, the baby boom was under way, and cities were expanding as never before. With automobile ownership growing rapidly, it became possible for more and more people to live beyond the reach of public transit. This fact, combined with the increasing disposable incomes that meant bigger houses were affordable, gave rise to suburban sprawl.

Voices 1940–1949

Canada's failure to accept more than a few of the Jewish refugees from
the Holocaust represents one of the sorriest chapters in our history.
Mark Sorensen, the man in charge of the Canadian Pacific Railway
immigration office in Copenhagen, became increasingly outraged
by the turning away of even the most qualified applicants – if they
were Jewish. In the late spring of 1940, following the closing of the
Copenhagen office, Sorensen, himself an immigrant to Canada, expressed
his feelings in a letter to a sympathetic fellow railway official.

Short only of treason We have come to the end of a
chapter in our Canadian immigration. It is now too late to amend
our ways to recover opportunities lost – and rare opportunities
we had these last six years – but we may well give thought to it,
consider where we ourselves have failed, and the forces working
against the movement to Canada of qualified people who were
in so urgent need of the refuge we could have offered them...
I cannot consider myself a Free Lance, but if I were I should
make this the biggest wartime scandal in Canadian Public Life
short only of treason...That the cause of this war is partly
owing to maldistribution of population you will not dispute,
but Mr. Blair and our Mr. Little would not understand, nor
would they see Canada's responsibility or the cards they for
years were putting into the hands of Hitler and Mussolini.

Mark Sorensen
1940

Hugh MacLennan's first published novel, *Barometer Rising*, followed
two failed attempts to write books with an international setting. It
marked a watershed in Canadian literature, being the first major work
in English set naturalistically in a Canadian place and time: Halifax
at the time of the great explosion of World War I. For the novel,
MacLennan drew extensively on his own boyhood in Halifax – he was
ten at the time of the disaster. Here one of his characters observes
the private study of the shipping magnate Geoffrey Wain.

Something proper and fitting Now that the room was
empty, he was forced to admit that it fascinated him. The Wain
house represented an aspect of Nova Scotia he had formerly
seen only from the outside, for he had been born in a farmhouse
in Cape Breton...Murray's eyes wandered from the map of
Jamaica to the rest of the room. The tables were heavy with
mahogany and the curtains the colour of ox blood; there were
four models of sailing ships, all reproductions of famous
Nova Scotiamen which had once been laded at the Wain wharf.
It did not seem to Murray a gracious room, yet there was something proper and fitting about it, and it had dignity. There were
no late-Victorian frills. At this moment in its silence he could
hear the rhythmic pulsating of the fog signals coming in from
the harbour which had given this old house its reason for life.

Hugh MacLennan
1941

Kotoma Kitagawa had arrived in Canada in 1926 with her Canadian husband Kensuke, who had made a journey to Hiroshima solely to acquire a bride. The couple set up a dry-cleaning business in Duncan, British Columbia, on Vancouver Island. They also ran a taxi business, which shuttled Japanese workers to and from the logging camps, and a small grocery store. When Canada declared war on Japan, her life suddenly changed.

We felt surrounded We spent four months, many days without knowing anything about tomorrow. We secluded ourselves in the darkened house with the windows closed. Since there were not too many Japanese around, we felt surrounded by white people and, in fact, they did watch us carefully. They informed on us to the police, saying for instance, that 'Kitagawa left home in the early evening,' and so on. They would watch from behind curtains...

Kotoma Kitagawa
1942

On the twentieth of April we arrived in Hastings Park. It was surrounded by barbed wire. We had to line up in the dining hall, holding a tin plate in our hands, wanting to cry from shame. At first I couldn't swallow the food. I was so sad to be there like a beggar while *hakujin* watched us from outside the fence. But to survive, we had to eat.

The great literary critic Northrop Frye developed a body of scholarly work that did much to define the Canadian consciousness as it emerged from colonialism. In the 1930s, he began contributing articles to *The Canadian Forum*, a journal of which he eventually became editor and in which the following appeared in 1943.

Truly Canadian Now admittedly a great deal of useless yammering has been concerned with the "truly Canadian" qualities of our literature, and one's first instinct is to avoid the whole question. Of course what is "peculiarly our own" is not what is accidentally our own, and a poet may talk forever about forests and prairies and snow and the Land of the North and not be any more Canadian than he will be Australian if he writes a sonnet on a kangaroo...Nevertheless, no one who knows the country will deny that there is something, say an attitude of mind, distinctively Canadian, and while Canadian speech is American, there is a recognizable Canadian accent in the more highly organized speech of its poetry. Certainly if a Canadian poet consciously tries to avoid being Canadian, he will sound like nothing on earth. For whatever may be true of painting or music, poetry is not a citizen of the world: it is conditioned by language, and flourishes best within a national unit. "Humanity" is an abstract idea, not a poetic image.

Northrop Frye
1943

Mary Pickford's natural screen presence and brilliant gift as a mime brought her international success as an actress in silent pictures, but she sensed that the uncomplicated innocence of her silent screen persona wouldn't survive the transition to the talkies, of which she made but four. After retiring in 1933, she refused to allow any of her films to be reissued or shown on television. By the end of her life she lived as a virtual recluse in her California mansion. In Canada, however, as she recollected in her memoirs, she never stopped being a celebrity.

Call me sweetheart **I was back in Toronto as guest of honor to eight hundred young World War II aviation cadets. Everything was all right till they began singing, "Let Me Call You Sweetheart." Then I looked out over the hall at the bright, ruddy faces of these young men soon to go overseas, some never to come back, others to wish they hadn't; it was more than I could bear. Despite my firm resolution and the overgenerous mascara on my eyelashes, the tears started rolling down my cheeks. And how the mascara stung my eyes and nose! I can only say, in all humility, that it is good to have lived to know that after so many years off the screen, there were young men, soldiers soon to embark perhaps on their last journey, who could still pay me the sweetest and most gallant compliment of all – to ask to be called their collective sweetheart.**

Mary Pickford
1945

By the end of 1946, nearly 50,000 war brides and their children had arrived in Canada. Many received a rude awakening from romantic fantasies of life in a promised land. Some found that their "husbands" had returned home to Canadian wives and families. A few fled back to Europe, but most gritted their teeth and stuck it out, like the woman who told her story to the editors of *Blackouts to Bright Lights*.

I started to cry **When I did get into Vancouver all dressed up, there was nobody to meet me, and I started to cry. I knew I was pregnant, and I thought Bob was married to someone else, or had a girlfriend and didn't want me. I was terrified. The Red Cross nurse came to me and gave me a cup of coffee. Someone said, "We should phone the other station," and sure enough Bob was waiting for me there. I was supposed to come on the CPR and I came on the CNR.**

 I didn't know what to expect when I came to Canada. I thought I would see cowboys. The prairie seemed so flat, it just went on for miles and miles. I couldn't believe it was such a vast country or that it was all one country…The first thing I bought in the store in Vancouver was this big doll for myself. I took it home and said, "Bob, this is for the baby." He said, "It's kind of big for a baby, isn't it?"

Margaret Brown
1946

Malcolm Lowry completed work on his one great book, *Under the Volcano*, after he moved to Dollarton, British Columbia, in 1940. Lowry was plagued throughout his life by alcoholism and paranoia, as is the main character in his masterpiece, the consul, who has this to say about the fair city of Vancouver.

Mine the country and quit **Suppose you land in Vancouver, as seems reasonable. So far not so good. McGoff didn't have much use for modern Vancouver. According to him it has a sort of Pango Pango quality mingled with sausage and mash and generally a rather Puritan atmosphere. Everyone fast asleep and when you prick them a Union Jack flows out of the hole. But no one in a certain sense lives there. They merely as it were pass through. Mine the country and quit. Blast the land to pieces, knock down the trees and send them rolling down Burrard Inlet.**

Malcolm Lowry
1947

W.O. Mitchell worked at a number of jobs during his lifetime, including lifeguard, farm hand, door-to-door salesman, stunt driver for a carnival, deckhand on a Greek steamer, high school English teacher, and editor of *Maclean's* magazine, but he made his mark with novels that portray the power and beauty of life on the prairies, above all the instant classic *Who Has Seen the Wind*, first published in 1947. The book's runaway success allowed him to quit teaching high school in High River, Alberta, and begin writing full time.

Up into the sky **"This is your prairie," Brian said.**
 The boy did not answer him. He turned and walked as silently as he had come, out over the prairie. His walk was smooth.
 After the boy's figure had become just a speck in the distance, Brian looked up into the sky, now filled with a soft expanse of cloud, the higher edges luminous and startling against the blue. It stretched to the prairie's rim. As he stared, the gray underside carded out, and through the cloud's softness was revealed a blue well shot with sunlight. Almost as soon as it had cleared, a whisking of cloud stole over it.
 For one moment no wind stirred. A butterfly went pelting past. God, Brian decided, must like the boy's prairie.

W.O. Mitchell
1947

The Newfoundland referendum was bitterly fought and split the province in two. Those opposed to union with Canada played on ancient fears and prejudices. Two referendums would be necessary before Newfoundlanders opted for Canada – by a narrow margin of 52 percent to 48 percent – in July 1948, and anti-Confederation sentiment would persist for many years.

The Hero of '48
(Sung to the Air of "A Mother's Love")
A fisher boy was leaving and going to Labrador,
Fishing the same old trap-berth where his father fished before,
And as he was leaving his mother, while standing on the quay,
He threw his arms around her neck, and this to her did say:

Anti-Confederation song 1948

Chorus

Don't vote Confederation, and that's my prayer to you;
We own the house we live in, likewise the schooner too;
But if you heed Joe Smallwood, and his line of French Patois
You'll be always paying taxes to the men in Ottawa.

...From Blanc Sablon to Chidley is owned by Newfoundland –
The rivers, bays, and coastlines, back to the height of land;
We won it in a lawsuit from Quebec years ago,
But now they hope to get it back with the tricks of Schemer Joe.

Chorus...

In 1948, Paul-Émile Borduas was teaching at the École du Meuble in Montreal when he joined with a group of Montreal artists known as the *automatistes* to publish *Refus global*, an attack on the art establishment that called for complete freedom of artistic expression. (The *automatistes* hailed from a variety of creative disciplines, including painting, literature, and drama, but all advocated the cultivation of unpremeditated art.) Borduas's authorship of the title piece of the manifesto, first published in 1948 in an edition of 400 mimeographed copies, got him fired from his teaching job but enhanced his reputation as a leader of the Quebec avant-garde.

Refus global
Fuzzy intellects began to clear, stimulated by contact with the *poètes maudits* who were not monsters, but dared to express loudly and clearly those things which the most unfortunate among us stifled out of shame and a fear of being swallowed alive. These poets shed some light by their example. They were first to acknowledge the anxieties of a modern world as painfully lost as a babe in the woods. The answers they brought were disturbing, incisive, fresh, altogether different from the tired old refrains heard in this land of Quebec and in seminaries the world over.
    The bounds of our dreams were changed forever.

Paul-Émile Borduas 1948

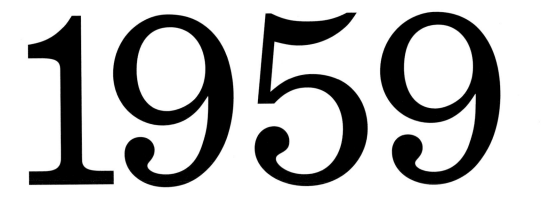

The Big Boom "'Apples! Peaches! Pears! And plums! Tell me when your birthday comes! January! February! March! April!...'

"We skipped all the time. My friends Debbie and Sue were better skippers than I was, they could even skip double-dutch. So I ended up turning rope a lot. I was better at hopscotch, so I always wanted to play hopscotch. Jacks was fun, too. But mostly it was skipping. That, and arguing about who was better, Buddy Holly or Paul Anka.

"Anyway, one day Debbie had just come back from summer vacation, and she came running over. Her family had gone camping in the States, and they brought back Hula Hoops! They got them shopping on the way back. We had heard about them on TV and everything, but you couldn't get them here yet. Debbie's family was like that. They were first on our block to have television. Before we got ours, our family used to go over and watch hockey or *The Wonderful World of Disney* in their rec room.

"So we had this huge Hula Hoop party in the street. Even the boys wanted to try. Even Jan and Anna Nagy came over and watched. They were new in the subdivision, D.P.s from the Communists or something. Their mom didn't speak English at all.

"Nobody could keep the hoop up! We didn't know it was going to be so hard! Arms and legs were easy, but that was cheating, it had to be around your hips. We shook like crazy and laughed and laughed. We just couldn't do it!

"You know what happened then? My mom came out, and Debbie's mom. And my mom took off her apron and took

one of the hoops. And she could do it! That hoop just floated around her waist, and she kind of waved her arms in the air. My mom and Debbie's mom turned out to be the Hula Hoop champions of the neighbourhood. She said it was from all the dances she used to go to with Dad before we were born. Neat!

"They were laughing like us kids, and when the ice cream man came around, my mom let us get Nutty-Buddies. They cost more than Popsicles, and she was pretty strict about that most of the time. Then some of the big kids started to get the hang of it, and Mom went in to get dinner going.

"Anna Nagy was chalking out lines for hopscotch, and I went over. That's when we first started being friends. She wasn't a very good skipper either."

In the hard times, you had delayed marriage, put off raising families, postponed new homes, tightened belts. Then hard times eased into the stable, prosperous 1950s. You could get out of school and find a real career. You could marry and start a family.

And you could hope for more: new electric appliances, and convenience foods with new wonder ingredients, and homes to put them in. In the 1950s, people moved into subdivisions where new houses were going up, hundreds at a time. Mothers stayed home with the kids while fathers commuted along new highways in shiny Fairlanes and Biscaynes. Immigrants began to arrive again, mostly from Europe. A Canadian population that had barely been replacing itself grew by 50 percent in the 15 years after the end of the war.

Visions 1950–1959

1950 April As the decade began, Canada looked as confident as this University of Toronto physics professor lecturing on the properties of liquid air. NATO defence ministers met in The Hague, Netherlands, where they agreed on a plan of collective self-defence against Soviet aggression. The idea for North Atlantic Treaty Organization originated in the Canadian Department of External Affairs and was first promoted in 1947 by Louis St. Laurent, external affairs minister at the time. The treaty was signed in 1949. Canada's first-ever peacetime military alliance grew out of self-assurance as well as Cold War jitters.

1950 July William Lyon Mackenzie King lying in state in the Hall of Honour of the Parliament Buildings. In what remains the most remarkable political career in Canadian history, King was Liberal leader from 1919 to 1948 and prime minister for almost 22 years. But he left behind a country whose new-found prosperity had failed to reach many, including the native people of the Canadian North, where malnutrition was often the norm. *Right:* A starving Padleimiut mother consoling her child at a camp on South Henik Lake, Northwest Territories.

1950 May In Winnipeg, the flooding Red River drove 100,000 people, including these two nuns, from their homes and caused $125 million in property damage – but only one death. "I remember seeing a small cottage floating down the river," one Winnipegger recalled. "It struck a bridge pillar and the furniture popped out one end as it opened like a cardboard cereal box." Every spring Manitobans have anxiously watched the rising waters. Despite the construction of a massive water diversion channel after another bad flood in 1966, one of the worst inundations on record took place in the spring of 1997.

1950 December Canadian troops arrived in South Korea as part of a United Nations force under the command of General Douglas MacArthur. Seasoned war correspondent René Lévesque, here interviewing Canadian troops for Radio-Canada International, sent home affecting reports from homesick members of the Van Doos Regiment. The war, which had begun in late June with the invasion of the South by the Communist North, took a dangerous turn when MacArthur sent troops across the line into North Korea, bringing Red China into the fray and raising the spectre of a much wider conflict.

1951 April Maple Leaf defenceman Bill Barilko (falling) scored the winning goal at
2:53 of overtime in game five of the Stanley Cup playoffs against Montreal. This famous
photo captures the moment the puck has beaten goalie Gerry McNeil but before the
transfixed fans have realized that Toronto has won the Stanley Cup, four games to one.
The 1951 series still stands as the only one in which every game was decided in overtime.
As for Barilko, he disappeared during a fishing trip that summer and was later memorialized
in 1992 in "Fifty Mission Cap," a song by the Tragically Hip.

1951 November The National Ballet of Canada gave its first performance, which included *La Sylphide.* Founded by British expatriate Celia Franca, seen here during a rehearsal (seated in foreground), it took on its "national" label without official mandate – a classic case of chronic Toronto-centrism. It was as if the older and already distinguished Royal Winnipeg Ballet, also founded by English expats, didn't exist. Under Franca's tutelage the National would become one of the world's premier classical ballet companies.

1952 January Canada's first homegrown governor general, Vincent Massey (*left*). If the country had an aristocracy then the Masseys were its cream, as suggested by this popular saying from earlier in the century: "In Canada there are no social classes, just the Masseys and the masses." The firm Vincent's grandfather had built exported farm machinery all over the world from its headquarters in Brampton, Ontario. Massey-Harris was of no use at all to Saskatchewan farmers battling an outbreak of foot-and-mouth disease that required the slaughter of 1,300 cattle (*above*).

1953 September *La famille Plouffe* premiered on the brand-new French CBC Television network (*top*). It premiered on English CBC the following year. Based on the novel by Roger Lemelin, *The Plouffe Family* unreeled the multigenerational saga of a family of the 1950s and soon became a fixture on Wednesday nights at 8:30 p.m. Television fed the rise of consumer culture and helped promote a taste for modern style in everything from cars to furniture (*above*).

In a generation, Canadians had evolved from scrimpers and savers into conspicuous consumers. Across the country, strip malls and shopping centres began to appear. Increased spending power meant higher demand for everything from TV dinners to detached suburban bungalows complete with crabgrass. And more young people, like the ones kicking up their heels above, could afford the extravagance of formal attire for their high school or college proms.

1953 Summer The epidemic of poliomyelitis, or polio, reached its peak, handicapping the futures of 8,000 Canadian children such as this toddler at a Sudbury clinic (*left*). A very different epidemic, the Red Scare, had begun to erupt in Canada in 1945 when Igor Gouzenko, a Soviet cipher clerk, had defected in Ottawa. Eight years later, the conviction of Americans Ethel and Julius Rosenberg for passing atomic secrets to the Soviets roused protests such as this one in Montreal, where demonstrator Mel Doig was arrested (*above*). The Rosenbergs maintained their innocence but were executed in 1953.

1953 July The Stratford Shakespearean Festival opened in a huge tent in a small Ontario town with a production of *Richard III*, starring Alec Guinness and directed by Tyrone Guthrie. Toronto *Globe and Mail* drama critic Herbert Whittaker hailed the event as "the most exciting night in the history of Canadian theatre." But neither the Stratford Festival nor the National Ballet nor the important regional theatres such as the Manitoba Theatre Centre, which opened in 1958, would have much outlasted the decade without the Canada Council, created in 1957.

1954 September Some called it the high point of the decade. When 16-year-old Marilyn Bell (here pictured during an attempt to swim the Juan de Fuca Strait between Vancouver Island and the mainland) was pulled from Lake Ontario, exhausted after swimming the 51.5 kilometres from Youngstown, New York, to Toronto in 20 hours, 59 minutes, she captured both headlines and hearts. Bell was perfectly cast in the role of 1950s heroine: polite, clean-cut, clean-spoken, and self-deprecating. Others would swim faster and farther, but none would catch the Zeitgeist so nicely.

EATON'S OF CANADA
SALUTES A CANADIAN ACHIEVEMENT

PROGRESS IN *BETTER* LIVING

1954 March The building of the Toronto subway, Canada's first underground transit system, here chronicled in photographs mounted in an Eaton's store window to celebrate the opening, took five years and cost $54 million. As the suburbs burgeoned, car sales skyrocketed. In 1956 Canadians bought 400,000 automobiles, a remarkable number in a country of 15 million. When the decade was done, they had purchased more than 3.5 million new vehicles and moved into 1.1 million new homes.

1954 October Destruction and construction coincided uncannily in Toronto in 1954, with the devastation wreaked by Hurricane Hazel coming so soon after the opening of the new subway. Hurricane Hazel lasted only a few hours but cost $24 million. The damage was soon repaired and Toronto became the fastest-growing city in North America, outpacing even Houston and Los Angeles, with huge fortunes made by homebuilders who seized the moment.

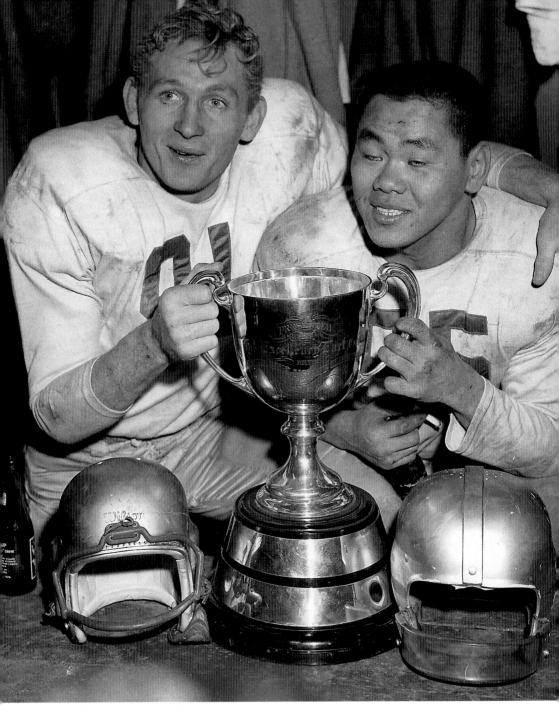

1954 April In the 1950s Canadian sports professionals played uniquely Canadian games, whether they hailed from Flin Flon or, like Jackie Parker (*above,* left), from Knoxville, Tennessee. The Edmonton Eskimos quarterback, here holding the Grey Cup with rushing great Normie Kwong (*above,* right), was undoubtedly the most popular man in Alberta for having mastered the three-down Canadian game, then leading his team to three successive Grey Cups in 1954, 1955, and 1956.

1955 March National Hockey League president Clarence Campbell suspended Montreal
Canadiens star Maurice "Rocket" Richard for attacking a linesman, triggering the worst
sports riot in Canadian history. The next game at the Forum had to be halted when a
tear gas bomb exploded on the ice. Fans threw eggs at Campbell, then went on a rampage
through downtown Montreal. Richard, of course, was more than a sports hero: he was
an emblem of Québécois achievement, so the incident took on ugly anti-English overtones.

1955 June Claude Jodoin (*left*), president of the Trades and Labour Congress of Canada, attending a Windsor convention. The next year the TLC and the Canadian Congress of Labour merged to form the Canadian Labour Congress. In the 1950s, Canada seemed to be advancing on all fronts. It took part in joint NATO exercises (*top left*), poured money into nuclear research (*top right*), and supported foreign aid projects like the Colombo Plan (*lower right*) while celebrating medical advances such as the pioneering work on human stress done by Hans Selye (*lower left*) in Montreal.

1956 September Except for the 1950s fashions, this Montreal lunch counter could have been lifted out of the 1930s or 1940s. But times were changing and, with them, tastes and values. As newly affluent citizens poured into Canadian cities, whose populations increased dramatically, they wanted to acquire many of the novel products recently brought to market, from transistor radios to portable barbecues to hairspray and instant cake mix. For teenagers, the focus was on pleasure, not rebellion, with conformity the prevailing style.

Girls wore white blouses and bobby socks; boys dressed in V-necked sweaters with white T-shirts. Only daring girls pierced their ears; only adventurous boys wore their hair in a ducktail. In fact, Claude Bissell, then president of Carleton University, expressed concern that his charges weren't rowdy enough. "I'm worried that not a single Ottawa resident has written me complaining of the activities of my students. Maturity is all right, but what I fear is premature senility." He needn't have worried. Everything was about to change.

1956 December At a convention in Ottawa, the Progressive Conservative Party chose John George Diefenbaker to succeed George Drew as party leader. A prairie populist and political maverick, Diefenbaker on the hustings (*opposite*) could be a spellbinding speaker, his sentences "like eggs rolling on a table, unpredictable, circumlocutious, errant, creating their own suspense," in the memory of a young Dalton Camp, who compared Dief's podium presence to that of a magician.

"Dief the Chief" wasn't the only person to cast a mass spell in the middle of the decade. American rock-and-roll sensation Elvis Presley mesmerized a generation barely born when Diefenbaker was first elected to Parliament in 1940. In April 1957, "Elvis the Pelvis" appeared in a $10,000 gold lamé suit before thousands of screaming and fainting fans in two sold-out shows at Maple Leaf Gardens (*opposite, top*). Ontarians seeking more religious forms of inspiration made the pilgrimage to Hamilton, Ontario, in July 1956 to experience the healing powers of American evangelist Oral Roberts (*opposite, lower photo*).

1957 June Prime Minister Diefenbaker and his just-sworn-in cabinet basking in the first Tory victory since 1930 (*top*). Dief made political history by appointing the first woman cabinet minister, Ellen Fairclough, then going on to win the 1958 election by the greatest majority ever. He accomplished the latter feat despite facing the new Liberal leader, Lester Pearson (*above left*, with his wife, Maryon), who had just won the Nobel Peace Prize for his role in solving the 1956 Suez Crisis. Vincent Massey (*above right*), a lifelong Liberal, read the Speech from the Throne, which promised lower taxes and higher old age pensions.

It wasn't long before the often-erratic leader got himself into trouble. One of Dief's most controversial decisions was the cancellation of funding for the Avro Arrow (under construction, *top*) a ground- and sound-barrier-breaking fighter jet that promised to revolutionize Canada's aerospace industry. Diefenbaker was most proud of his Canadian Bill of Rights, which proved noble but ineffective. Pierre Elliott Trudeau, still a Montreal writer and lawyer in the late 1950s (*above*, with union leader Gérard Picard), would eventually champion the stronger Charter of Rights and Freedoms. **297**

1957 May Piano prodigy Glenn Gould (*top left*) played in Moscow and Leningrad. Gould wasn't the only Canadian artist gaining an international reputation in the 1950s. Mordecai Richler (*top right*) had already published his second and third novels from his new home in London, England. (His first book sold a mere 200 copies in Canada.) Ottawa photographer Yousuf Karsh (*above*) had made "Karsh of Ottawa" a household name. But the average Canadian, asked to pick a homegrown superstar, would have named Paul Anka (*right*), the Ottawa native whose monster hit "Diana" topped the charts in 1957.

1958 March CBC Television star and the original Canadian songbird, "Our Pet, Juliette," striking a publicity pose (*right*). Juliette's show aired each Saturday night from 1956 to 1966 following *Hockey Night in Canada*. With government support for Canadian culture, it was a golden time for both popular and serious entertainment. Dora Mavor Moore, here visiting the New Play Society theatre school she had founded (*above*, at right), nurtured many actors and playwrights and founded the long-running satirical review *Spring Thaw*.

1958 February Diefenbaker appointed the first native senator, James Gladstone (*top*, at left, with friends at the Blood Indian Reserve north of Cardston, Alberta). At 71, Gladstone was old enough to remember the Boer War, some of whose veterans (*left*) gathered in Montreal to watch a memorial parade that year. In most ways the world these men had been born into had long vanished – but certain aspects of Canadian life remained grimly familiar. In November, 39 miners (*above*, one being laid to rest) died at Springhill, Nova Scotia, in one of the country's worst below-ground disasters.

1959 June Queen Elizabeth II opening the St. Lawrence Seaway as her husband, Prince Philip, and U.S. Vice-President Richard Nixon and his wife, Pat, looked on. President Dwight D. Eisenhower, who also spoke at the ceremony in Saint-Lambert, Quebec, called the seaway "a magnificent symbol to the entire world of the achievements possible to two democratic nations peacefully working together." But Canada and the United States, joint administrators of the system, would often quarrel over how it should be run.

The seaway replaced old and antiquated canals and locks with new systems that permitted modern bulk freighters to travel throughout the Great Lakes. It drowned historic villages along the St. Lawrence River, but its beneficial effects were felt from the huge iron-ore deposits of Quebec and Labrador to the far-inland grain terminals of Thunder Bay. In its first three months, 1,875 ships passed through its locks.

1959 Autumn "The Beatnik Kiss" by photographer Kryn Taconis freezes a fleeting
poetic moment known as Beat Culture, an import from its birthplace in San Francisco.
Beatnik writers and artists like Toronto painter Gordon Rayner (seated at right)
frequented coffeehouses and listened to jazz and folk songs while using a new slang
that included words such as "dig," "bad scene," "cool," "groovy," and "something else."
The Beat may soon have faded, but it was a portent of tumult to come.

A Quebec nun contemplating the soon-to-be-opened airport at Dorval near Montreal. As the decade came to a close, the economic boom seemed unstoppable while the baby boom was at its peak. Elvis was still king and Ottawa's Paul Anka was still Canada's hottest pop music export with "Put Your Head on My Shoulder." Ontario's tenth university, York, was formed. A Quebec company called Bombardier produced the first Ski-Doo, and Canada's first French-Canadian governor general, Georges Vanier, moved into Rideau Hall.

Voices 1950–1959

In 1950, Pierre Trudeau, Gérard Pelletier, and a group of young Quebec intellectuals opposed to Maurice Duplessis and the Union Nationale founded *Cité libre*, a journal that sought to define the liberal, modern, anti-nationalist Quebec society they hoped would emerge from the Duplessis era. One of Trudeau's earliest *Cité libre* pieces, published in 1950, suggests the high moral tone of much of the writing within the journal's pages.

We also have to do good
It is not enough to avoid evil; we also have to do good. A church would be an impostor if it stayed forever in the catacombs. Similarly, in politics, you cannot stay below ground too long. An excess of unhappiness will snuff out the spirit, and heroic resistance will degenerate into beast-like stubbornness. That unfortunately is what happens to some people who struggled too much, and take virtue itself to be a negation.

Pierre Elliott Trudeau
1950

Both American and Canadian football derive from English rugby, but they differ in significant ways. The Canadian game features a longer and wider field with deeper end zones and calls for 12 players to a side as opposed to the American 11. These physical facts, combined with only three downs instead of four, make for the more wide-open, pass-oriented Canadian game. This letter about the virtues of Canadian football appeared in *Saturday Night* in November 1950.

A grand game
There is something to be grateful for at this time of year in the fact that there is at least one great and popular game in Canada which can depend upon her own resources. Rugby football continues, and we hope long will continue, to be a different thing from the football of any other country. The Canadian can say to himself, "My football right or wrong, but always my Canadian football." It is true that we seem to be borrowing a few players from south of the border, but the contribution that they bring us is mostly weight and muscle, articles which can be produced anywhere with the proper diet and exercise. The rules, the technique, and above all the enthusiasm of the game, these are our special property, not to be shared with any other country. This is all to the good. In too many other matters, Canada is a bit too much of an appendage to one or other of two large countries with which we have close connections...But Canadian football is a grand game and our own...Long may it reign.

Anonymous
1950

In 1951, the Ontario legislature passed "An Act to Ensure Fair Remuneration to Female Employees," which is excerpted here. By the end of the decade, all provinces, except Quebec and Newfoundland, had adopted similar legislation. Upon passage of the act, Ontario Premier Leslie Frost commented, "This is indeed a historic day in Ontario; women are being given completely equal status with men."

Other than sex

An Act to Ensure Fair Remuneration 1951

(1) No employer and no person acting on his behalf shall discriminate between his male and female employees by paying a female employee at a rate of pay less than the rate of pay paid to a male employee employed by him for the same work done in the same establishment.

(2) A difference in the rate of pay between a female and a male employee based on any factor other than sex shall not constitute a failure to comply with this section.

After serving in World War II, Farley Mowat spent two years in the Arctic, an experience that led him to write his first book, *People of the Deer*. Like most of his writing for adults, it is largely auto-biographical and expresses deep empathy for the dispossessed, in this case the caribou-hunting Ihalmiut people. The book had a huge impact, but Mowat later felt some remorse about its influence: "The government saw to it that no Eskimo died of malnutrition and the medical services were improved and nobody froze to death. But they turned the whole of the Canadian Arctic into a charity ward."

A trivial gift

Farley Mowat 1952

A trivial gift Ohoto was smoking his little stone pipe, a tiny and shapely object of semi-translucent stone, neatly and artistically bound with the brass from an old cartridge case. I said good-by to him in the white man's way, and after we had shaken hands he took the pipe from his mouth and, without speaking, handed it to me. It was a trivial gift in farewell. And yet – how trivial was it? I knew how that pipe had come down from a century that is gone, for it was the pipe of Elaitutna, Ohoto's father. It had seen more of the land and more of the things in the land than any man living had seen or would see. It was to have gone with Ohoto into his grave, to remain with him as a familiar thing in the eternity he sought at the end of his days. Now it would go with me, instead, out of the land, to lie warm and smoldering in the palm of my hand as I remembered the things I needed to say if the voices of the Ihalmiut were to be heard in the world of the Kablunait.

Before Charles Vincent Massey became Canada's first native-born governor general in 1952, he held many important posts, including Canadian high commissioner to Great Britain. But he left his most lasting legacy as chair of the Royal Commission on National Development in the Arts, Letters, and Sciences – the Massey Commission – which in its 1951 report recommended the formation of the Canada Council. In an address to the Canada Club of London on Dominion Day 1953, Massey explained his rationale for government support of the arts.

They have things they must say I am aware that

the true artist is one who has something to say or to show; and that, if he is a true artist, he will show it or say it without thought of reward. I am equally convinced that the true artist, consciously or not, must draw his inspiration and insight from the society in which he lives; he cannot talk if no one will listen. In Canada today the important thing is that so many young people trained in literature or in our other languages – painting, music, sculpture, drama – feel that they have things they must say, and that people will listen. This is their concern; not to produce a Canadian masterpiece but to speak, to be heard, and to be understood.

Vincent Massey
1953

Even into the early 1950s, the Toronto art scene was still dominated by the Group of Seven, a situation intolerable to young painters who wanted to see abstract painting recognized and exhibited in Ontario. Eleven of these artists – Jack Bush, Oscar Cahén, Hortense Gordon, Thomas Hodgson, Alexandra Luke, J.W.G. Macdonald, Ray Mead, Kazuo Nakamura, William Ronald, Harold Town, and Walter Yarwood – banded together to form Painters Eleven. Their first group show at the Roberts Gallery in 1954 attracted big crowds but garnered no sales. Elements of their philosophy are outlined below.

A universal language In the war of sound (not sight)

that surrounds painting today, we hear of a vast and conclusive return to nature, as if nature were a bomb shelter to be used in time of plastic trouble. We are nature, and it is all around us; there is no escape, and those who wish to go back have nowhere to go. What might seem novel here in Ontario is an accepted fact everywhere else. Painting is now a universal language; what in us is provincial will provide the colour and accent; the grammar, however is a part of the world.

Painters Eleven
1957

The humble characters of Gabrielle Roy often experience the human condition as an intermittent and unpredictable series of joyous moments in a less than wonderful life. Roy, who was born in St. Boniface, Manitoba, set several of her books in the French Canada of the West. One of her Western novels, *Rue Deschambault*, excerpted here, won both the Prix Duvernay and the Governor General's Award.

To prevent a marriage

Mother and I were rolling along in a train toward Saskatchewan, on our way there to prevent a marriage...We had been in the train for quite some time. Maman was seated facing me, her hands on her skirt, unaware of the passing countryside. She must have been going over it in her mind what she would say to my big sister Georgianna. I had never seen much of Georgianna, who, the very year I was born, had gone to teach school in Saskatchewan. There was a photograph of her at home. Her hair was done up in two heavy black braids, tied with a ribbon above her ears, and in this picture she had excessively eloquent eyes. Even in a photograph, Georgianna looked as though she were ready to jump up and say, "Here I am!..." and then burst into laughter at everyone's surprise.

Gabrielle Roy
1957

In 1957, John George Diefenbaker swept the Liberals from office after 22 years of uninterrupted rule, bringing a breath of fresh prairie air to stale Ottawa politics. In those heady days, before the weight of office and the perceived betrayal of former adherents soured the taste of victory, the 61-year-old prime minister wrote to his mother, Mary, as he had almost every day of his adult life when they were apart.

A wonderful life

My dear Mother,
    When you receive this it will be my birthday and I'll be in P.E.I. and I'll be thinking of you. 62 years ago is a long long time and I have had quite a wonderful life – and all of it due to you and father. I often think of how we would strut if he were living. He used to talk so much of those "stern, proud men" who were Ministers of the Crown when he was in Ottawa and saw them so close at hand from the Gallery. But of all the years this last one has been the most unbelievable. Mr. Drew didn't resign until the 25th Sept. – so it isn't a year ago yet since things began to move and yet in a few days I will have been in office for 3 months. But there are no more honors to acquire for me since the Queen made me an Imperial Privy Councillor yesterday – so now my job is to do well. Well, Mother, you will be only 22 years older than me for the next 5 weeks.
    You are not so old, are you – or am I?
    With lots of love and good wishes – and no words to express what I owe to you.

John Diefenbaker
1957

John

Mordecai Richler's novels often attempt to cast outwardly contempt-ible characters in a sympathetic light. The following is from *The Apprenticeship of Duddy Kravitz*, Richler's fourth and best-known book, published in 1959, which proved him to be a major novelist at the tender age of 28. *Duddy Kravitz* is one of a series of Richler novels that explore the Jewish ghetto around St. Urbain Street in Montreal. It follows the life of a young hustler struggling to escape the ghetto.

A man without land is nobody

Mordecai Richler
1959

"Do you trust me, Yvette?"

"Yes."

"I want to buy this lake."

She didn't laugh.

"I'm going to build a children's camp and a hotel here. I want to make a town. Ste Agathe is getting very crowded and five years from now people will be looking for other places to go."

"That's true."

"A man without land is nobody," he said.

Yvette felt that his forehead was hot and she made a pillow for him out of a towel.

"If the wrong person saw this place he might get the same idea. That's why you mustn't tell anyone we came here or bring anybody else here. Who owns the land, Yvette?"

Brault owned a third of it, maybe. She wasn't sure about the rest. Brault was a hard man to deal with.

"So am I," Duddy said. "And this land is mine."

The Canadian clothing design industry was in its diapers during the 1950s, with Canadian taste in women's attire both conservative and derivative. The following reminiscence, published in the book *Remembering the '50s*, describes an attitude to female fashion that now seems antediluvian.

Those garter belts
We wore reversible plaid skirts. They were sewn down on the hips and showed a different plaid when you wore it reversed. And I remember the little furry pom-poms on a velvet rope that you tied around your neck. Hair rollers – I spent a lot of time in rollers. And nylons. That was one of the big parts of growing up. I remember those garter belts. And a girdle, you had to have one of them. Our Home Economics teacher told us, "Girls, as soon as you have anything that wiggles, that's the time to get one of those little girdles." We were about fourteen then. She also told us that the back of the knee was the ugliest part of the female anatomy. That, of course, determined your skirt length.

Anonymous
circa 1959

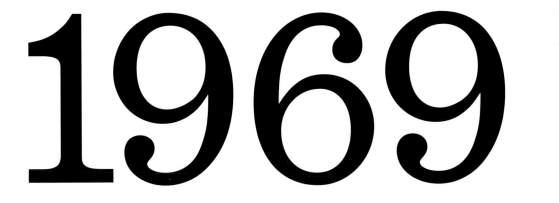

Turbulent Identity

"I was walking out by the chemin Queen-Mary on Sunday, and around a corner I almost bumped into a row of nuns. They were walking all in a line, silent, holding rosaries. They were wearing the old habits – not like some of the sisters now – all black, covering the head and right down to the ground. Just for a moment I was back home, coming in from the farm to the *école paroissiale*, and being led off to Mass in long lines like that.

"I haven't felt that way since I finished the secretarial program and came to my sister's here in the city. I cried two days, I was that scared. Then at the *pharmacie* I bought Miss Clairol. It was new then. I went blond, just to be a new person, you know? I found a job – 'Help Wanted, Female' – with a company that was building a piece of the Métro. Business was good, they could afford to let me learn on the job. The pay was nothing much, but I could stay in the city, find a little room for me.

"The city! Montreal! The city then, it seemed so alive. Everyone was so stylish, so chic. Robert Charlebois's music was playing everywhere. The girls in mini-skirts were going to the discothèque and the cafés all the time, not like home. It was the new Québec. I wanted to be part of that. It was only in the English *quartier*, the big stores, that I didn't feel at home so much.

"At Christmas, the office had a big party and, well, I slept with the boss after. Later I found he tried that with all the secretaries. I felt so guilty. Not because he was the boss; we didn't think that way then. Because he wasn't my husband. But maybe I liked it, too?

"What if I was pregnant? I wasn't, but when I left

that job and was on the *chômage* a few weeks, I read some pamphlets that this new organization, the Fédération des femmes, handed out. It talked about the pill and why couldn't women get divorces. Abortion, I could not say the word. I had never heard of liberation for women, all that was new then. But I could understand when they said I would be paid better if I was a man. Some of the things they said, I felt that 'click' they talk about.

"Later, I worked as a secretary at the new CEGEP downtown. The boyfriend I had then was an activist in the union, and in the Mouvement souveraineté-association, maybe even in some organizations he didn't talk about. We started going to rallies and marches. Through him I was active in sovereignty, and I started to believe things could change, we could have the world we wanted. I joined the women's caucus, and I kept on there even after I was not with him.

"But I almost forgot to tell you about the song. It was in the Expo summer. I went with some friends to a concert on the Expo islands. It was maybe for the Fête nationale, the Saint-Jean-Baptiste. And the star was Pauline Julien.

"She took my breath away. I was still just a little girl from outside Saint-Hyacinthe, you know. And Pauline Julien, she was one of us. She was Québécoise, and she was a woman. She was so strong and so proud. I don't sing, but I turned to my friend and I said, 'I want to be her.'

"I guess I still want to be her. That keeps me going forward. In a couple of years, I think, we will be a nation. I think of it like that. Like Pauline Julien singing 'Gens du pays' at the Expo concert, with fireworks up behind her over the river, and all of us swaying together and singing."

Visions 1960–1969

1960 November Outside a Toronto burlesque theatre, reporter Robert Thomas Allen looked inquiringly at striptease artist Ann Howe. Canadians may have regarded strippers as risqué at the beginning of the decade, but burlesque, with its roots in vaudeville, looked almost quaint in view of the lightning transformations and social upheavals of the "Swinging" Sixties. A mere seven years later at a restaurant/bar on the Yonge Street strip, lunchers would be permitted a pause between mouthfuls to apply paint to the body of a seated young woman wearing nothing at all.

1960 December Hockey legend Gordie Howe (*opposite*) got his 1,092nd point, to become the NHL's all-time leading scorer. By the time Howe retired at age 52 – and not including his six seasons in the WHA – he had nearly doubled this total to 2,010, a mark that has been exceeded only by Wayne Gretzky. Other aspirants to sports immortality included Ann Heggtveit (*above left*), who captured Canada's first skiing gold, and 21-year-old Bobby Hull, pictured pitching hay on the family farm near Point Anne, Ontario (*above right*).

1960 December Canada welcomed the 2-millionth immigrant to arrive since the end of World War II. In a nation largely populated with newcomers, Canadians' attitudes towards immigrants had always been ambivalent: sometimes welcoming and assimilating new arrivals eagerly, just as often fearing and shunning alien faces and alien ways of life. Immigration policies had often been racist and exclusionary.

John Diefenbaker's government, for all its loyalty to the "British connection," opened
Canada's doors to non-British immigrants. In 1960, immigrants from Britain still made
up the largest single group, but the second-largest came from Italy, among them the family
pictured here. In subsequent decades multicultural immigration would transform
Canadian society.

1960 August The Inuk artist known simply as Kenojuak (*top*) who made her most famous work, *The Enchanted Owl*, at Cape Dorset, Baffin Island, that year, said that she drew her images "out of my thoughts, and out of my imagination... I am not trying to show what anything looks like in the material world." The same year, Robertson Davies, here attending the rehearsal of one of his plays (*left*), joined the faculty of Trinity College at the University of Toronto. Davies, with his perfectly rounded sentences and Edwardian mien, couldn't have been more different from the brash Montreal poet Irving Layton (*above*).

1961 May In Ottawa, President John F. Kennedy and his wife, Jacqueline, were greeted by Prime Minister Diefenbaker and his wife, Olive, on Kennedy's first state visit to Canada. Even more than her charismatic husband, Jackie wowed the 50,000 people who lined the route of the Kennedy cavalcade, signalling the birth of Jackiemania. The visit also set a nasty tone for Canada–U.S. relations. JFK injured his back during a ceremonial tree-planting and later told his aides that he found Diefenbaker "boring." The PM never forgave him. He called JFK a "boastful son of a bitch."

1961 August At the founding convention of the New Party (*above*), Tommy Douglas
(*top left*) was elected leader. The new political formation, soon to become the New Democratic
Party, was forged of an alliance between the Co-operative Commonwealth Federation (CCF)
and the Canadian Labour Congress. Douglas, who had pioneered the Canadian welfare
state – including medicare – during his 17 years as Saskatchewan premier, would lead the
NDP until 1971. Also in 1961, socialist and former Quebec CCF leader Thérèse Casgrain
(*top right*) founded the Quebec chapter of Voices of Women to protest nuclear testing.   **327**

1962 Summer Tourists wandering among totem poles on the campus of the University of British Columbia in Vancouver. What had represented heathen ways to early European settlers, who tore down totems and banned the potlatch, now helped foster a West Coast tourist boom. The settlers' descendants viewed the art of the aboriginal peoples of the Pacific Northwest as a high point of world indigenous culture. And the massive totem poles that recorded both myth and genealogy were seen as artistic masterpieces.

1962 September With the opening of the 45-storey Royal Bank Building, the first phase of the Place Ville Marie development, Montreal got a landmark in the modernist International Style that was about to transform the downtowns of Canada's major cities. The building, designed by American architect I.M. Pei, is cruciform, so as to admit natural light to every interior space. Before Place Ville Marie was completed in 1965, the Toronto Dominion Centre, designed by leading modernist Ludwig Mies van der Rohe, would be under way. In 1968, Calgary's 190-metre Husky Tower would open.

1962 September Canada became only the third nation in space with the launch by NASA of *Alouette*, our first orbiting satellite, part of an aerospace boom that included this radio telescope (*top left*) at the Dominion Astrophysical Observatory in Penticton, British Columbia. Back on the ground, Eaton's opened its first suburban outlet in Toronto (*top right*). Meanwhile, Canadians were learning to live better electrically, with the help of this General Electric display at the Canadian National Exhibition (*above*).

On the work front, the word processor remained a gleam in some inventor's eye, but women working in steno pools like the one pictured here (*top left*) could now tap away on electric typewriters. The Canadian economy remained heavily resource-based. Mining at the world's largest potash reserve in Saskatchewan (*top right*) began in September. And in Newfoundland outports fishery workers were still drying cod the same way it had been dried for centuries (*above*).

1962 November With 9 minutes and 22 seconds left to play, the fog at the Grey Cup game between the Hamilton Tiger-Cats and the Winnipeg Blue Bombers got so thick that the electronic scoreboard disappeared. The "Fog Bowl" was called with the score 28–27 in favour of the Bombers. When the remaining minutes were played out the next day, the score stood.

1963 May The Quiet Revolution got noisy when a series of bombs exploded in mailboxes inside the Montreal Anglo enclave of Westmount. This latest bomb attack by the newborn Front de libération du Québec (FLQ) came just a few weeks after the Liberal government of Lester Pearson took office and less than a year after the re-election of Quebec's Liberal government under the slogan "Maîtres chez nous" ("Masters in our own house").

In its first two years, the government of Jean Lesage (*above*) had swept away the old world of Quebec politics represented by the Union Nationale under Maurice Duplessis. Among the Lesage government's most notable achievements were the secularization of the education system and the nationalization of hydroelectricity – the brainchild of Lesage's combative minister of natural resources, René Lévesque. Despite, or perhaps because of, the rapid pace of change in Quebec, separatism also gained momentum and radical adherents.

335

1964 May In Lexington, Kentucky, Northern Dancer (*above*, right), owned by tycoon
E. P. Taylor, became the first Canadian-bred horse to win the Kentucky Derby. Northern Dancer,
winner of the Queen's Plate, went on to win the Preakness but came third in the Belmont
Stakes, thus missing the coveted Triple Crown. But his exploits won him an unprecedented
honour when he became the first horse elected to the Canadian Sports Hall of Fame.

1964 June Motorists cruising along the Trans-Canada Highway, opened officially in 1962 with the completion of the difficult Rogers Pass section through the Rockies. Construction on the world's longest continuous highway had begun in 1949 (and continued until 1970). These years saw the height of North American car culture, when the new models from Detroit were launched each fall to great excitement. Three years later, the Canada–U.S. Auto Pact would confirm a single North American market for automobiles. Nissans, Toyotas, and Hondas from Asia were just entering the Canadian market.

1964 June Demonstrators crowded Parliament Hill (*above left and right*) as the Flag Debate began inside the House of Commons and, with extraordinary passion, across Canada. Should Canada have "its own" flag? Or did the Red Ensign, featuring the Union Jack in the corner and the fleurs-de-lis in its crest, best represent a country with such strong British roots and an undeniable French fact? After the prime minister proposed his own design – a spray of three red maple leaves flanked by vertical bars of blue that was instantly dubbed the "Pearson Pennant" – hundreds of competing suggestions flooded in from across the country.

Finally an all-party committee settled on a compromise that pleased almost no one but soon came to seem as inevitable as the snow in winter. The passion of the debate seemed as hard to fathom as the Beatles hysteria that greeted the first visit to Canada by the Fab Four that summer (*top, far left to right*). If the mop-toppers (*top right*) seemed calmer, it was because they were trying so hard to be cool.

1964 January Canadian artist Michael Snow, here posing in his Big Apple studio (*above*), showed his *Walking Woman Works* at New York's Poindexter Gallery. Clearly the Maple Leaf flag wasn't the only new Canadian look as the decade neared its midpoint. At poet Irving Layton's Montreal wedding (*top left*), Leonard Cohen sported a fashionably skinny tie as he charmed a well-coiffed woman. But 1960s style could seem a throwback to the 1950s. Just look at the bouffanted belles (*lower left*) in their formal get-up at Montreal's Place des Arts. No wonder Snow was so fascinated by the iconography of the feminine. **341**

1965 January President Lyndon Johnson (*above*, right) took Prime Minister Lester Pearson for a ride at the LBJ Ranch in Johnson City, Texas, before the two signed the Canada–U.S. Automotive Agreement, or Auto Pact. Pearson oversaw a period of great change, launching the Royal Commission on Bilingualism and Biculturalism and backing his minister of health and welfare, Judy LaMarsh (*top left*), in her drive to create the Canada Pension Plan. *Top right:* Ookpik, a big-eyed doll from Inuit craft cooperatives, enjoyed a brief fame in Canada and abroad.

1965 Spring As Kryn Taconis's remarkable photograph of deaf children undergoing vibration therapy at a school in Milton, Ontario, implies, attitudes towards the deaf and other "disabled" people were beginning to change as more and more attempted to take a full part in mainstream society. At the World Games for the Deaf that spring, Canadian JoAnne Robinson broke several swimming records.

1966 March Justice Minister Lucien Cardin dangled before the press an allegation about a spy named "Olga," and Canada had its first political sex scandal. Olga turned out to be Gerda Munsinger (*top left*), a German prostitute who'd had an affair with Pierre Sévigny while he was a minister in Dief's last cabinet and was delighted to talk about it on CBC's national TV news. The popularity of the nightly newscast was rivalled only by *Front Page Challenge* (*above*), which at its peak pulled in 2 million viewers each week.

One of *FPC*'s early guests was Canada's most famous Soviet defector, Igor Gouzenko (*opposite, top right*), who always wore his hood in public, even when promoting one of his several best-selling books. The panel regulars were Gordon Sinclair, Betty Kennedy, Charles Templeton, and Pierre Berton, here being stumped by Malcolm X (*opposite*). Media guru Marshall McLuhan (*above*), who would publish *The Medium Is the Massage* in 1967, preferred the "hot," information-dense medium of radio to the "cool" information-starved medium of television, which he argued was damaging our way of perceiving the world.

1967 April Prime Minister Pearson (at far right) welcomed into his cabinet Pierre Elliott Trudeau, John Turner, and Jean Chrétien. This picture is remarkable in that it portrays one sitting prime minister and the next three Liberal ones. Pearson would soon announce his resignation, and the neophyte justice minister, Trudeau, would abruptly find himself the favoured successor. This changing of the guard occurred against a backdrop of social upheaval unprecedented in the postwar period, but whether Trudeau, already almost 50, could harness the energy of the youth revolt remained to be seen.

In 1967, protests against the war in Vietnam were reaching their peak (*opposite, top left*) and the culture of youth protest was at its zenith. Bob Dylan's concert in Vancouver (*opposite, top right*), where clean-cut Robbie Robertson (at right) played backup, left good vibes in a city already awash with hippie culture (*top left*). And Toronto's Yorkville Avenue (*top right*) had been transformed from a sleepy residential street into a throbbing counter-cultural hub.

347

1967 Summer Something happened to Canadians during the centennial year of
Confederation. Cynicism and self-doubt vanished, and we felt good about ourselves and
our country. The focal point for this outpouring of national pride was Expo 67, the
six-month-long World's Fair in Montreal. Even as cool-headed a cultural critic as Robert
Fulford waxed unrestrained: "Expo 67 was the greatest birthday party in history,"
he wrote, "but for those willing to learn it was also an education. For one beautiful,
unforgettable summer, Expo took us into the future that can be ours."

The tensions between French and English evaporated in the sunlight of international acclaim, making the impossible dream of a bicultural utopia seem just around the corner. The fair itself, whose theme was a catch-all "Man and His World," added up to much, much more than the sum of its parts. Its crazy quilt of futurist structures rising from two islands, one artificial, in the St. Lawrence River somehow worked. No one seemed to mind the endless lineups for the most popular pavilions, including Buckminster Fuller's striking geodesic dome (*above*), housing a wild assortment of American cultural artifacts.

1967 July Expo euphoria burst with the four words uttered by French President Charles de Gaulle (*above*) from the balcony of Montreal City Hall: "Vive le Québec libre!" Mayor Jean Drapeau, a staunch federalist, was not pleased; Pearson denounced the speech, but the damage was done. When a Montreal gang attacked a Centennial event in September and an ugly fight with the RCMP ensued (*left*), it was easy to blame the mischief on de Gaulle. Incidents like this one helped give Trudeau the Liberal leadership in 1968: English Canada saw him as a strong federalist who could "keep the French in their place." **351**

1968 Spring While the counter-culture produced anti-fashion, women who wanted to be in style piled their hair high, like this spectator consulting the racing forms at Edmonton's Northland Race Track (*above left*). Hemlines too went higher and higher. This "entertainer" at a club in Ontario's uranium mining capital, Elliot Lake, may not have been radioactive but she was clearly making sparks fly (*above right*). Her mini-skirt wasn't far off the mainstream fashion of the era. The only element missing was the go-go boots.

1968 April Trudeau (*above*) won the Liberal Party leadership on the fourth ballot, beating out a strong field that included business candidate Robert Winters and Paul Martin (*top, being interviewed by Pierre Berton*), who'd been in Louis St. Laurent's cabinet and helped design the national health care system. Trudeau seemed to fulfill a Canadian yearning for a Kennedyesque leader. But the suave exterior concealed a certain ruthlessness. Within days of his victory, he called an election, denying outgoing prime minister Pearson his cherished chance to bid farewell to the House of Commons.

1968 Winter Boxer George Chuvalo regained the Canadian heavyweight title by defeating Jean Claude Roy. Chuvalo, who had battled Muhammad Ali through 12 rounds but failed to dislodge the world champion, became a quintessential Canadian hero by never getting knocked down. The same year, Michel Lambeth took this haunting picture of a woman injecting herself with heroin (*right*). Commenting on his most memorable photographs, Lambeth wrote, "They are, in a way, analogues of terse poetry, images which give up their message very quickly without pretense of gimmick, subterfuge or flippancy."

1969 Fall As the decade drew to a close, the Guess Who (*above*) rocketed onto the world scene with the aggressively sexist and baldly anti-American hit "American Woman." But then anti-Americanism was all the rage. Anti-war protesters filled the streets of Canadian as well as U.S. cities, and American draft dodgers crowded our proliferating sidewalk cafés.

One of the more creative anti-war demos was staged by this group of students (*top*), who enacted a parody of the program of "rural pacification" practised by American troops in Vietnam. The village being pacified here is Frelighsburg, Quebec. In December, Pierre Trudeau cemented his claim to the trendiness crown by meeting with John Lennon and his wife, Yoko Ono, in his Parliament Hill office (*above*). The famous Beatle spent 40 minutes closeted with the prime minister – "five minutes longer than he'd spent with heads of states," Lennon reportedly gushed.

Voices 1960–1969

Marshall McLuhan liked to describe himself as first and foremost a grammarian, but it was his analysis of the grammar of mass media that made him famous. He coined the terms "global village" and "the medium is the message" in his provocative if not always intelligible attempts to explain how the rise of electronic technology – especially television – was changing the way people thought and how they perceived the world. The following passage is taken from his 1964 essay "Murder by Television."

Since TV

Since TV The TV child cannot see ahead. Why? Because he is too deeply involved in his perceptual modes. Since TV, gone is the speedy, superficial habit of youth in a visually organized world. Today the young are earnest, serious, obsessional. Since TV, they are "with" things. They "dig" situations…Since TV, that is to say, our children have tried to get *inside the page*. They demand a new relation to the typographic form that they have carried over from their depth involvement in the TV image. The results are most unfortunate, visually, psychically, and pedagogically. Print and TV clash *as forms*.

Marshall McLuhan 1964

Margaret Laurence found her literary voice when she imagined the town of Manawaka, based on her birthplace, Neepawa, Manitoba. The following excerpt is from *The Stone Angel*, the first of her four Manawaka novels, now considered one of the high points of Canadian writing. The book paints a moving portrait of Hagar Shipley, a woman torn all her life between her overwhelming zest for life and her puritanical upbringing. At 90 years of age, Hagar attempts to maintain some dignity in the face of the ravages of terminal illness.

Care to pray?

Care to pray? We remain in heavy silence, Mr. Troy and I. I glance at him and see he's struggling to speak and finding it impossibly difficult. He thinks me formidable. What a joke. I could feel almost sorry for him, he's perspiring so. Stonily, I wait. Why should I assist him? The drug is wearing off. My bones are sore, and the soreness is spreading like fire over dry grass, quickly, licking its way along. All at once, an eruption of speech, Mr. Troy bursts out.

"Would you – care to pray?"

As though he were asking me for the next dance.

"I've held out this long," I reply. "I may as well hold out a while longer."

"You don't mean that, I'm sure. If you would try – "

He looks at me with such an eagerness that now I'm rendered helpless. It's his calling. He offers what he can. It's not his fault.

"I can't," I say. "I never could get the hang of it. But – you go ahead if you like, Mr. Troy."

Margaret Laurence 1964

In 1963, Liberal leader Lester B. Pearson had promised a distinct flag for Canada if he was elected. But his first moves to keep the promise in the spring of 1964 were met with howls of outrage from many quarters, among them the Canadian Legion. In mid-May, less than a month before the Flag Debate was to begin in the House of Commons, Pearson flew to Winnipeg to address the legion's annual convention. During his speech he recalled his own military service in World War I.

Canada ahead of its parts
I had as comrades in my section, men whose name were: Cameron, Kimora, English, Gleidenstein, de Chapin, O'Shaughnessy. We didn't fall in or fall out as Irish Canadians, French Canadians, Dutch Canadians, Japanese Canadians. We wore the same uniform, with the same maple leaf badge, and we were proud to be known as Canadians, to serve as Canadians and to die, if it had to be, as Canadians... What we need is that soldierly pride in Canada, that confident, passionate pride in Canada, that men had who wore the uniform with the maple leaf badge on it. What we also need is a patriotism that will put Canada ahead of its parts. We are all or should be Canadians – and unhyphenated; with pride in our nation and its citizenship, pride in the symbols of that citizenship. The flag is one such symbol...

*Lester Pearson
1964*

In the 1960s, it was difficult to open the newspaper without seeing Pierre Berton's byline or to turn on the television set without seeing his face. And this was before the first book of his massive two-volume saga of the Canadian Pacific Railway, *The National Dream* (1970), made him the country's leading purveyor of popular history. If Pierre Berton had an opinion, it was worth listening to. In 1965, when he published his attack on the complacency of modern clergy, *The Comfortable Pew*, it set tongues wagging from coast to coast.

A comfortable creed
Why is it that the Church today is afraid to speak loudly and with a radical voice? Perhaps it is because the Church, like so many of its members, is afraid to look ridiculous. It ought to be making front-page headlines regularly by advocating what is absolutely counter to the general thrust of society; but it does not do so. How many Christian ministers today go to jail for their beliefs? How many make the kind of physical protest that puts them outside the bounds of the social order?...The institution of religion, which once generated its own values, now merely gives its blessing to the majority-held values of the community around it...

Institutional Christianity, in short, has become a comfortable creed, a useful tool for Peace of Mind and Positive Thinking, a kind of sugar-coated pill that soothes those who fear to face the traditional Christian concerns of evil, suffering and death...

*Pierre Berton
1965*

With the passage of Bill C-187 in 1967, divorce no longer required proof of adultery. Most important, the new law permitted divorce on the grounds of "marriage breakdown." The bill was drafted by Justice Minister Pierre Trudeau's predecessor, Lucien Cardin, but Trudeau's speech in defence of the bill ensured its passage. He argued, "The concepts of the civil society in which we live are pluralistic and I think this parliament realizes that it would be a mistake for us to try to legislate into this society concepts which belong to a theological or sacred order." These were the bill's grounds for divorce.

To render intolerable A petition for divorce may be presented to a court by a husband or wife, on the ground that the respondent, since the celebration of the marriage,

Divorce Act
1967

(a) has committed adultery;

(b) has been guilty of sodomy, bestiality or rape, or has engaged in a homosexual act;

(c) has gone through a form of marriage with another person; or

(d) has treated the petitioner with physical or mental cruelty of such a kind as to render intolerable the continued cohabitation of the spouses.

George Woodcock, one of Canada's major men of letters, espoused the view that society's best interests were served by individuals not affiliated with any formal government organization, which may explain his attraction to the Doukhobors and their uneasy relationship with outside authority. The following passage is from *The Doukhobors*, which Woodcock wrote in collaboration with Ivan Avakumovic. The book did much to quell the sensationalist portrait painted by the media, which focused on the nude parades and violent acts perpetrated at the turn of the century by the radical Sons of Freedom. In the following passage they burn the house of the sect's moderate leader, Peter Veregin (also written Verigin).

The nakedness of holy poverty While the leader was at Brilliant, Alex Makhortov, one of the heroes of the first nude march, led a score of chanting men and women to the big octagonal house Peter had built at Verigin. They set it on fire and then stripped off their clothes, threw them into the leaping flames, and stood singing hymns while the Community Doukhobors angrily whipped them and summoned the Royal Canadian Mounted Police. The motives of the act were clear. Verigin's house represented the material things of this world. By burning it, the Sons of Freedom were doing him a kindness, since they were divesting him of corrupting material possessions; but they themselves, in performing the act, were also symbolically renouncing wealth, and as a sign of this they threw the clothes they were wearing into the flames and stood in the nakedness of holy poverty.

George Woodcock
1968

Judy LaMarsh is remembered as a member of the Liberal government of Prime Minister Lester Pearson. As minister for health and welfare, LaMarsh was responsible for the Canada Pension Plan. She also laid the groundwork for Canada's medicare system, and as secretary of state she brought in the Broadcasting Act and presided over Canada's Centennial Year celebrations. *Memoirs of a Bird in a Gilded Cage* (1968) tells the story of this remarkable political pioneer.

Without enough women

Judy LaMarsh
1968

The dirty jobs of politics, the ones of no glamour, often fell to me. Like a good soldier, I did my part. Women are much more realistic about this than men – we know that much of life is made up of dirty, tough jobs, that someone has to do. Someone has to clean off a sticky bottom when a diaper needs changing, someone has to wash the cold eggy plates, flick off the accumulated dust, and look after sick people. Women understand that men must often be kept from soiling themselves with the little dirty details of life in order to accomplish the big shiny jobs unimpeded. And women in politics have generally accepted this role – to do all the hum-drum, tedious, must-be-done jobs. Pity the party without enough woman power – there will always be dreamers and leaders, but the dreams won't come true, nor will the leaders reach their goal, without their ready-doers.

Margaret Atwood once described Gwendolyn MacEwen's poems as "brilliant and original verbal surfaces." MacEwen's sense of the relationship between poetry and history contributed greatly to the strength of her work and helped her win two Governor General's Awards. Both in her poems and in her fiction she explored the worlds of dream and magic. "Dark Pines under Water" originally appeared in MacEwen's 1969 collection, *The Shadow-Maker*.

Dark Pines under Water

Gwendolyn MacEwen
1969

**This land like a mirror turns you inward
And you become a forest in a furtive lake;
The dark pines of your mind reach downward,
You dream in the green of your time,
Your memory is a row of sinking pines.**

**Explorer, you tell yourself this is not what you came for
Although it is good here, and green;
You had meant to move with a kind of largeness,
You had planned a heavy grace, an anguished dream.**

**But the dark pines of your mind dip deeper
And you are sinking, sinking, sleeper
In an elementary world;
There is something down there and you want it told.**

Harold Cardinal's 1969 polemic, *The Unjust Society*, was written in reaction to the controversial government paper titled "The Statement of the Government of Canada on Indian Policy," which proposed the abolition of special rights for native peoples. In his book, Cardinal argues in favour of retaining special rights for natives within the context of a strengthened infrastructure of Indian organizations, treaties, and government legislation.

Extermination through assimilation **The new Indian policy promulgated by Prime Minister Pierre Elliott Trudeau's government, under the auspices of the Honourable Jean Chrétien, minister of Indian Affairs and Northern Development, and Deputy Minister John A. MacDonald, and presented in June of 1969 is a thinly disguised programme of extermination through assimilation. For the Indian to survive, says the government in effect, he must become a good little brown white man. The Americans to the south of us used to have a saying: "The only good Indian is a dead Indian." The MacDonald-Chrétien doctrine would amend this but slightly to, "The only good Indian is a non-Indian."**

Harold Cardinal
1969

Flower power arrived in Canada via the West Coast, where in the late 1960s Vancouver's *Georgia Straight* managed to offend just about every establishment sensibility. In Toronto, the counter-culture made its headquarters at Rochdale College, which billed itself as an experiment in "free" education when it opened in a highrise on Bloor Street in 1968. Zipp Almasy, a former *Georgia Straight* staffer working on the Rochdale security crew, also wrote for a local rag called *Harbinger*. Here he imagines what would happen if a cartoon hippie named Acidman became prime minister.

A just society **The age of consent will be lowered to twelve years, birth control pills will be given to all females age 12 or over, hallucinogenic drugs will be government inspected and sold in drug-stores, pornography will be legalized, churches will pay taxes, jails will close down and criminals will be treated in hospitals, underground papers will receive government grants – pass the joint – all cities will be required to open at least one public beach for nude bathing, the police will be disarmed, homosexuality will be legalized, welfare and unemployment insurance will be increased, discrimination on any grounds will be punished, gambling, abortion, and prostitution will be legalized and taxable, censorship will be banned, each city will set up digger-houses, suicide will be permitted, sex education will start at kindergarten, students will govern schools and universities...yes, it will indeed be a just society.**

Zipp Almasy
1969

Compassion and Conviction
"Martin and I got together on my last trip up to Yellowknife with the deputy minister. Now there is a guy stuck in the past. I mean, I'm grateful, but he's really rigid, you know.

"It started with Martin down in Kitsilano when I was just back from CUSO in '72. I had a grant to finish my dissertation. But after two years seeing socialism in East Africa, I wasn't quite ready to settle down and become a prof. Martin had hustled up a LIP grant for a social infrastructure project out of Fort St. John.

"I said, Far out, in Tanzania I had been thinking about their *ujamaa* model for rural socialism. We put our stuff in the back of Martin's pickup and we were gone. I knew I was really back in Canada when we watched Paul Henderson's goal in a pub in Prince George.

"They had a commune a few miles out of the Fort, some Yank war protesters and some local freaks in two big old houses and a couple of geodesic domes. Had a patch of weed back in the bush, of course.

"Martin and I drove all over, trying to get on as advisors to the Indian reserves. But they were more interested in his pickup truck. We would spend a day explaining rural socialism, and one of the elders would say, 'Maybe we should go to town,' and about nine people would pile in the truck. Martin said he was learning. But I could see what the chances were of them hiring some white-kid consultants out of grad school.

"Martin spent time in the communities, but I hung out at the commune. Stan, one of the draft guys, was trying to start up a macrobiotic health-food co-op. Jane, his old lady then, was working on a novel. Then the Mackenzie Valley pipeline thing started up, and energy people were coming through the North. Martin kept in touch, and he introduced me to a guy who hired me to coordinate some environmental-impact reporting. I organized briefs for the Berger inquiry, and then I transferred to Energy, Mines and Resources in Ottawa. They were growing fast, what with the OPEC energy crisis. I got in on the Petro-Canada launch, and Sable Island gas, and conservation. Soon I was hiring old profs of mine on research studies.

"I arranged a leave and turned some of our work into a quick dissertation on public-sector energy initiatives. With that, I got a good spot in the assistant deputy minister's office. Since then I've hooked up with a lobbyist from one of the industry associations. She has a kid from her first marriage, and we have a house together in the Glebe. I've been laying out a model for national energy self-sufficiency, and the political guys in the minister's office want me to prepare a submission to Cabinet.

"Martin never did get himself out of the North. He's still listening to the wisdom of the elders. Now that he's in the Territories, he's involved with what they call the Dene Nation. When I saw him in Yellowknife, it was pretty obvious he thinks I'm gone over to the other side. Okay, it's a long way from the revolution we used to talk up, driving those endless highways in northern B.C. But with a strong energy policy initiative we could build something really special in this country.

"So I've done all right for myself, too. Do I have to apologize for that?"

Visions 1970–1979

1970 June Montreal women and their children marching in support of the legalization of abortion. In 1970, a physician convicted of performing an illegal abortion – legal only if the life of the mother was at risk – could be sentenced to life in prison. The modern women's liberation movement, born in the 1960s, came into its own in the 1970s. In the early 1960s the birth control pill had given women their first real sense of reproductive choice. The right to abortion was the logical if controversial next step.

1970 October The kidnapping of British trade commissioner James Cross on October 5 in Montreal by the Front de libération du Québec precipitated the October Crisis. On October 15, a second FLQ cell kidnapped the Quebec minister of labour and immigration, Pierre Laporte. The next day, after an appeal from Premier Robert Bourassa, the Trudeau government invoked the War Measures Act, a first in peacetime. The police gained the right of indiscriminate search and seizure (*top*) and of detention without charge, and 10,000 soldiers descended on Ottawa, Montreal (*above*), and Quebec City.

Civil libertarians protested against the use of the War Measures Act, but Parliament and the public overwhelmingly endorsed the government's action, especially after the body of Pierre Laporte was found in a car trunk on October 17 (*top*). When a reporter asked Trudeau how far he was prepared to go to fight against what he called "a parallel power which sets itself against the elected," he replied, "Just watch me." By the time Trudeau and Bourassa (*far right*) attended Laporte's funeral (*above*) on October 21, the FLQ's independence-through-terror project had lost public sympathy.

371

1970 October The coffin of Pierre Laporte entering Montreal's Notre Dame Church (*top*). As the crisis dragged on, over 450 people languished uncharged in Quebec jails. In December police found the FLQ cell holding James Cross and negotiated his release; four weeks later the Laporte cell was arrested and its leaders, Paul Rose (*above left*) and Jacques Rose (*above right*), gestured defiantly after being charged with kidnapping and murder. The movement for independence that had been so confidently expressed by this Saint-Jean-Baptiste Day celebrant (*right*) a few months earlier shifted into peaceful political activities.

1971 Summer Hippie culture continued well into the 1970s, especially at musical gatherings like the Mariposa Folk Festival (*left*), where such celebrities as Joni Mitchell, Neil Young, and Gordon Lightfoot were showered with love. In western Canada, there was no love lost for old-style politicians. In June, Allan Blakeney's NDP kicked out the Saskatchewan Liberal government of Ross Thatcher. In August, Progressive Conservative Peter Lougheed (*above*), here seen campaigning at Indian Days in Hobbema, Alberta, ended the Social Credit dynasty that went back to 1935.

1972 September Countless female fans supported P.E.T. on the campaign trail. A year earlier, Pierre Elliott Trudeau had become the first prime minister to marry in office when he wed Vancouverite Margaret Sinclair, a ravishing 22-year-old. Although Trudeau appeared to be settling down, his marriage only seemed to add to his sex-symbol status. As Geoff Pevere and Greig Dymond wrote, "If this gorgeous, free-spirited flower child could go for the PM – despite the chasm of age, experience, intellect and inclination between them – then we must indeed have had the coolest and sexiest leader on the face of God's earth."

1972 October Out recruiting support, the leader of the opposition, Conservative Robert Stanfield, appealed to more mature Canadian voters. Despite the different styles of the two party leaders, the November 1972 election was extraordinarily close and Trudeau won only a minority government. Stanfield, according to many "the best prime minister Canada never had," never came as close again. Intelligent, decent, and with a wonderfully wry sense of humour, he couldn't compete with Trudeau in the image-driven political context of the 1970s.

1972 September A class at Toronto's Gladstone Public School (*top*) celebrating the most famous goal in Canadian hockey history. In the net for Canada was Ken Dryden (*above*, at left), here standing with Alan Eagleson (*above*, middle), who had arranged the series. After losing the first game in Russia, the Canadian professionals appeared done for. But one-point victories in games six and seven set up the unforgettable final. The Soviets went ahead early; the Canadians stormed back. With only 34 seconds to play, Paul Henderson (*right*) put the puck into the net and himself into the Canadian sports pantheon.

1973 April When President Richard Nixon came to Canada to discuss the front-burner issue of water and air pollution, he and Prime Minister Trudeau signed the Canada–U.S. Great Lakes Water Quality Agreement. While Canada could justly claim that industries in the American border states were polluting the Great Lakes, Canadians were doing their share – especially when it came to acid rain. This nickel smelter in Sudbury, Ontario, was the single biggest source of acid gas emissions on the continent, and Canada's environmental laws were often weaker than American laws.

1973 August At Mururoa Atoll, French Polynesia, crew members of the Canadian Greenpeace ship *Rainbow Warrior III* were beaten by French sailors who boarded and seized their vessel during an anti-nuclear protest. By the end of the decade, Greenpeace was a leading force in ecological activism. The Canadian environmental movement's crusades of the 1970s included halting Spanish and Icelandic whalers in the Atlantic, keeping Russian fleets off the North American coast, and – with the assistance of French starlet Brigitte Bardot – fighting the seal hunt on Newfoundland ice.

1973 June Members of a wedding party crossing a field in Nova Scotia following the ceremony. Though Canadian urban life became more and more homogeneous with the ascendancy of television and mass-market advertising, century-old traditions persisted throughout the country. In the Maritimes, the first century of Confederation had witnessed a steady decline in economic power and influence. Nova Scotia, New Brunswick, and Prince Edward Island accounted for less than 5 percent of Canada's gross domestic product in the 1970s, down from 16 percent in 1890.

In an attempt to address economic disparities, the Trudeau government had initiated massive transfers of tax revenues from the richer provinces to the poorer ones. The program was administered by DREE, the Department of Regional Economic Expansion, but the only thing DREE expanded was the number of civil servants working in Ottawa. Despite 30 years of subsidizing the poorer regions at the expense of the more prosperous, Canada remains a country deeply divided between the haves and the have-nots.

1973 June The Parti Québécois won 30.8 percent of the popular vote in the Quebec election although it took only six seats. The results represented Quebec's growing endorsement of the moderate separatism of René Lévesque (*top*), here shown consoling PQ supporters. Not until 1976 would Lévesque become the first separatist premier of Quebec. Once in office, the PQ proved a competent government that expanded Bourassa's commitment to the massive James Bay hydroelectric power development (*left*), begun in 1971 despite protests over the uprooting of northern Cree like this couple (*above*).   **385**

1974 June Russian ballet star Mikhail Baryshnikov (*top left*, at right) at Ontario Place with colleagues Sergiu Stefanschi and David Haber after his defection while in Toronto with the Kirov Ballet. Baryshnikov soon joined the American Ballet Theatre but returned to Canada for guest appearances with the National Ballet, whose homegrown principals Karen Kain and Frank Augustyn (*top right*) were on their way to dance stardom, after taking top prize at a competition in Moscow the year before. Canadian singers were also making their mark in the world, notably Joni Mitchell (*above left*) and Anne Murray (*above right*).

1974 August Two men on the Bonaparte Indian Reserve near Cache Creek, British Columbia, saluting a slain comrade. In early August, about 20 natives set up a roadblock on a highway running through the reserve, charging a toll and enforcing it with loaded rifles. On August 22, 17-year-old David Roberts was killed in a confrontation with local police at the blockade site. Several of the blockaders wore the insignia of the American Indian Movement, whose quest for "Red Power" was spreading into Canada.

1975 January The United Nations proclaimed International Women's Year. The Canadian government commissioned John Reeves to photograph the changing faces of women across Canada. Among the subjects Reeves cast his lens upon: (*top row, left to right*) broadcaster Barbara Frum, homemaker Betty Lee, politician Rosemary Brown, author Margaret Atwood; (*bottom row, left to right*) author Margaret Laurence, Senate Speaker Renaude Lapointe, photographer Nina Raginsky, and singer Maureen Forrester.

"I think IWY was fantastic – it gave women an opportunity to look at themselves and the job they're doing," Sharon Batt, editor of the Edmonton-based women's magazine *Branching Out*, said that year. But she added, "Nothing took place that would encourage large numbers of women to enter the labour force." In 1979, Doris Anderson, president of the Canadian Advisory Council on the Status of Women, noted, "The fundamental fact that women at the end of the 1970s are still economically disadvantaged at every level of society means that the struggle for change must continue well into the 1980s and beyond."

1975 March Henry Morgentaler, surrounded by supporters, heading to prison to begin serving a sentence, after being convicted of performing an abortion without the approval of a three-person hospital committee as required by law. Later in the month, he would be released long enough to receive an award as Humanitarian of the Year. In 1973, a Montreal jury had acquitted Morgentaler of carrying out illegal abortions although he had admitted to more than 5,000. In 1974, the Quebec Court of Appeal overturned his acquittal and put him back in jail. At a new trial, a second jury acquitted him again.

1975 June Ed Broadbent, an autoworker's son and politics professor, was elected leader of the New Democratic Party. Here Broadbent is flanked by two members of the male old guard, outgoing leader David Lewis (left) and one of the CCF's founders, Stanley Knowles (right). The leadership race was a challenging one for Broadbent, who had to fight off a strong bid by Rosemary Brown, a well-known and well-respected feminist MLA from British Columbia. Accepting his party's mandate, Broadbent said that his goal was to convert democratic socialism into a workable political program.

391

1975 April The last piece of Toronto's CN Tower was fitted into place, completing the world's tallest free-standing structure. In the 1970s Toronto surpassed Montreal in both population and cultural importance.

1976 October Margaret and Pierre Trudeau swinging their two-year-old son Sacha at Vancouver airport before leaving for Japan. A year later the couple would part ways, and Trudeau would become our first single-parent prime minister.

1976 July "The Montreal Olympics can no more have a deficit than a man can have a baby," Mayor Jean Drapeau had famously declared, but by the time Queen Elizabeth opened the 21st Olympic Games in a new stadium, forever after to be known as "the Big O," it was already certain that the first Olympics held on Canadian soil would be a financial disaster. Drapeau's vain attempt to rekindle the flame of Expo 67 nonetheless proved to be a sports success and a media bonanza.

After the kickoff of the opening ceremonies (*opposite, top left*), the first week of the Olympics was marred by the withdrawal of most of the African competitors to protest the games' failure to expel New Zealand, which had recently sent a rugby team to play in South Africa. Still, the games went on. *Opposite, top right:* Olympians flying over the water jump in the steeplechase final. *Top left:* Members of the Canadian cycling team taking a turn around the track. *Top right:* The closing ceremonies were enlivened by a long-distance streaker.

1978 Spring A freestyle skateboard champion in Toronto showing off his style, using a gorilla grip to lift his board over a stack of five. Skateboarding, which began in California in the '60s, had by now become a sport only for the acrobatic. According to one veteran, "back in the '70s, freestyle skating meant tricks. Handstands, 360s, nose wheelies. 'Radical' meant pulling a 'coffin' at high speed. What's a coffin? Well, jump on your skate, lie down on your back, put your hands together like you're praying and you're doing a coffin."

1978 April Dairy farmers dumping milk on the steps of the Saskatchewan legislature in Regina to protest the federal government's refusal to provide subsidies for milk production. Canadian farmers had come to depend heavily on marketing boards that protected prices against international competition, a policy championed by Eugene Whelan, Trudeau's colourful agriculture minister. Whelan had faced irate Quebec dairy farmers on Parliament Hill a couple of years earlier and been doused for his courage. "If I'd been a dairy farmer, I would have been throwing milk too," he commented.

1979 August In Saskatchewan, as John Diefenbaker's funeral train neared the end of its long, slow journey from Ottawa, three generations of the George Jenzen family bade him farewell. Although ousted as leader and increasingly isolated within his party, Diefenbaker had stubbornly refused to bow out of Parliament, making life miserable for his successor, Bob Stanfield. His funeral – modelled after the funeral of Winston Churchill – was by far the most lavish and expensive state funeral in Canadian history. It had become the obsession of his declining years.

Regardless of how Canadians felt towards Diefenbaker as a politician and a person, he had become a mythic figure to millions. As Denis Smith wrote in *Rogue Tory*, "His legend was bigger and more generous than the man. For Diefenbaker himself, it seemed finally to offer a substitute for the failures he could not face. Yet he had a stubborn pride, and his long life turned into an epic. For Canada at mid-century, it was an undoubted act of virtue to embrace the legend of a leader who preached dignity and equality for all its citizens."

1979 May Pierre Trudeau finally lost an election as Joe Clark's Conservatives gained enough seats to form a minority government. Trudeau soon announced his retirement from politics, but nine months later Clark's government came to an end over its first budget and Trudeau came back to power. In July, a very different sort of end occurred, when over 50 pothead whales beached themselves on the rocky coast of Point Au Gaul, Newfoundland. The whales' mass suicide was a mystery for which scientists could offer no explanation.

1979 September In teen bedrooms across the country and on dance floors across the land, the sounds of the 1970s began to fade. The Guess Who and its offshoots were superseded by groups like Trooper, Prism, and Loverboy. Gino Vanelli now strutted before swooning devotees, while one of the best-selling records was Claudja Barry's "Boogie Woogie Dancin' Shoes," and disco diva Patsy Gallant hit the top of the charts, as disco clubs like Montreal's Douze 34 (*top and above*) got groovers into the groove.

1979 August Gilles Villeneuve at the U.S. Grand Prix, at Watkins Glen, New York (*left*).
He would win the race and maintain his rank as one of the world's most successful racecar
drivers, but his career was cut short in 1982 when he was killed at the Belgian Grand Prix.

1979 November More than 200,000 people were evacuated from Mississauga, Ontario,
after a CP freight train carrying dangerous materials jumped the tracks and began
leaking deadly chlorine gas (*above*). It was the greatest evacuation in Canadian history. **405**

Voices 1970–1979

As founder of the Parti Québécois in 1968, René Lévesque became the leading voice of moderate Quebec separatism, something he called sovereignty-association. On October 16, 1970, at the height of the October Crisis, he wrote an article in the *Journal de Montréal*, from which the following excerpt is taken.

A puppet of the federal rulers Quebec no longer has a government.

René Lévesque
1970

The stump of a one we did have was swept away at the first really hard blow. Bourassa's cabinet has turned in its hand and is no longer anything but a puppet of the federal rulers.

It is now clear that from the very beginning of this tragic period marked by the kidnapping of Mr. Cross, this government has only had a bit player's role. During the pseudo-negotiations initiated last Sunday by Mr. Bourassa, we were, alas, obliged to conclude that it had accepted to serve simply as the instrument of a policy conceived and determined outside its control; that it played the card of compromise while knowing all the time about the intransigent stand that was being taken in Ottawa; that in fact it was preparing the present climate by letting the situation drag on and grow rotten while pretending to ponder what to do; and, finally, that last night it was this government that backed the extreme move of the Trudeau regime in placing the whole of Quebec under military occupation until next spring...

Award-winning geneticist David T. Suzuki had just begun his television career in 1971, with the CBC program *Suzuki on Science*, when the Faculty of Science at the University of New Brunswick invited him to speak on "Genetics and the Future of Man." The speech, judging by this excerpt, shows that while Suzuki's rhetoric may have moderated somewhat over the years, his highly politicized approach to popular science remains intact.

A global imperialist A second aspect to survival in the next decade is that this is the American century. The United

David Suzuki
1971

States has dazzled the world with the gaudy plastic products of its powerful technology. It has been a global imperialist, it has infiltrated the political and economic structure of countries throughout the world, and ripped off gigantic pieces of the world's oxygen and resources while returning its wastes to the planet. If we in Canada are to survive at all, it will depend upon the fate of the United States of America. And all we can hope for over the next decade is that the radical and reactionary polarization will bring that system to a stop, or that its whole superstructure will collapse of its own weight.

When Glenn Gould wrote "Art of the Fugue" in 1972 he might just as easily have been writing about himself. The famously eccentric Canadian pianist had by then completely abandoned the concert stage for the recording studio, but his devotion to contrapuntal music and above all to the keyboard music of Bach remained undiminished.

Glaciated choruses Bach was forever writing fugues.

No pursuit was better fitted to his temperament and there is none by which the development of his art can be so precisely evaluated.

Glenn Gould
1972

He has always been judged by his fugues. In his last years, still writing at a time when the avant-garde of his day was occupied with more melody-oriented endeavours, he was dismissed as a relic of an earlier, less enlightened age. And when that great grass-roots Bach movement began in the early nineteenth century, his partisans were well-intentioned romantics who saw in those massive, glaciated choruses from the St. Matthew Passion or the B Minor Mass insoluble, if not indeed unperformable, enigmas, worthy of devotion primarily because of the faith they so triumphantly exuded. Like archae-ologists, excavating the substratum of a forgotten culture, they were impressed with what they found, but pleased primarily by their own initiative in finding it.

Margaret Atwood's first book of literary criticism, *Survival*, rode the wave of post-Centennial "Canlit" to surprising popular success. In it she takes an informal, even playful look at what it means to be Canadian.

Hanging on as a people The central symbol for Canada

– and this is based on numerous instances of its occurrence in both English and French Canadian literature – is undoubtedly Survival, *la Survivance*. Like the Frontier and The Island, it is a multi-faceted and adaptable idea. For early explorers and settlers, it meant bare survival in the face of "hostile" elements and/or natives: carving out a place and a way of keeping alive. But the word can also suggest survival of a crisis or disaster, like a hurricane or a wreck, and many Canadian poems have this kind of survival as a theme; what you might call "grim" survival as opposed to "bare" survival. For French Canada after the English took over it became cultural survival, hanging on as a people, retaining a religion and a language under an alien government. And in English Canada now while the Americans are taking over it is acquiring a similar meaning. There is another use of the word as well: a survival can be a vestige of a vanished order which has managed to persist after its time is past, like a primitive reptile. This version crops up in Canadian thinking too, usually among those who believe that Canada is obsolete.

Margaret Atwood
1972

When Premier Joey Smallwood retired, temporarily, from Newfoundland politics in 1972, he could truthfully claim to be the only living Father of Confederation. "We are not a nation. We are a medium-sized municipality...left far behind the march of time," he had told Newfoundlanders during the successful campaign for union with Canada in the late 1940s. In 1973 he published his autobiography, *I Chose Canada*, from which this excerpt is taken.

Ever-present danger

If I had advice to give to my successors in power, and to my fellow Newfoundlanders, it would concern the ever-present danger that threatens to destroy Newfoundland. We are so far removed from the corridors of power, so far from the massed population and power of Canada, so far from the main Canadian market, so much out of the minds of Canada's principal captains of industry and finance, that we could easily be wasted down the drain. It will require our most stubborn determination to defeat the force of megalopolis. Never say die! Never give in! Turn a deaf ear to the timid and faithless. And then at last, if the very fates do defeat us, go down, not with a whimper, but defiantly to the end. With that spirit there will be no going down.

Joey Smallwood
1973

Dennis Lee's most famous poem, "Alligator Pie," first appeared in *Wiggle to the Laundromat*, a collection of poems for children published in 1970. But only with the release of the bestselling *Alligator Pie* in 1974 did this seductive rhyme for pre-schoolers become a national addiction. It also guaranteed that his distinguished career as a serious adult poet would often be overshadowed by his celebrity with kids.

Alligator Pie

Alligator pie, alligator pie,
If I don't get some I think I'm gonna die.
Give away the green grass, give away the sky,
But don't give away my alligator pie.

Dennis Lee
1974

Alligator stew, alligator stew,
If I don't get some I don't know what I'll do.
Give away my furry hat, give away my shoe,
But don't give away my alligator stew.

Alligator soup, alligator soup,
If I don't get some I think I'm gonna droop.
Give away my beanie, give away my bloop,
But don't give away my alligator soup.

Dr. Henry Morgentaler was one of the first physicians in Canada to perform vasectomies, insert IUDs, and prescribe birth control pills to unmarried women. In 1973, he was charged under the Criminal Code and tried in Quebec after he announced that he had performed over 5,000 abortions. Found not guilty by a jury, Morgentaler was nonetheless ordered imprisoned by an appellate court judge, whose decision was upheld by the Supreme Court. Morgentaler made the following statement after learning in 1974 that the Supreme Court had upheld his initial conviction on Criminal Code charges.

My only regret I must now serve 18 months in prison, not because I have committed a crime, but because I cared enough to help women who asked for help, women who needed help, because I cared enough to protect their life and health. And if I go to prison it is with a good conscience, that in spite of all difficulties and stresses, and everything else, I probably saved a few hundred women from death, and maybe a few thousand from injury, humiliation, and stress. I have no regrets, my conscience is clear. My only regret is that, at this time, women in this country are still suffering, they are exposed unnecessarily to anguish, stress, and danger of death and injury because of a restrictive law, which in theory tells them that they can have an abortion if they need to, and in practice denies them this right.

Henry Morgentaler
1974

Barrie Phillip Nichol was a prodigious writer, editor, and performer, best known for his unconventional poetic structures and his antipathy to capital letters. He spent a lifetime exploring the form and syntax of speech, as he does in "Against Explanation," published in his 1974 collection *love: a book of remembrances*.

Against Explanation
oh the a be
an or and and
c

c d q o p
stops

whistle up gorge leg
laughter m l steep
la lune la lune

low l t s z
v v o b q r
la tigre i y w

 moon
june
spoon

bp Nichol
1974

Although he is best known for his fiction about baseball, especially the novel *Shoeless Joe*, W.P. Kinsella's first published book of fiction was *Dance Me Outside*, a collection of stories set on the Hobbema Reserve in central Alberta that featured a cast of native characters, including Silas Ermineskin and his friend Frank Fence-post. Through Ermineskin's eyes the white man's world is seen as a repressive and humourless place, in contrast to the spontaneous world of aboriginal people.

Panache His lecture was all about a French word called panache, which he say is, and I write it down real careful: *the ability to exude the effect of a plume on a helmet.*

W.P. Kinsella
1977

He show us pictures of knights with big curled feathers above their armour, and he tell us that anybody can act like he got them feathers. If we stand tall and have the right attitude then we can have panache and look like we warriors wearing a war bonnet and holding a lance, even if we really just got on jeans and a T-shirt. Then we look at pictures of Indian chiefs and Mr. Nichols say that they got more nobility and panache than knights ever had. I make sure I remember what it is he tells us but I don't figure I have a chance to use it for maybe a long time.

When Leonard Cohen was offered a Governor General's Award for his *Selected Poems* of 1968, he turned it down, a typically anti-establishment gesture by this poster boy of the Montreal literary avant-garde. By the time *Death of a Lady's Man* was published in 1978, Cohen had already begun the songwriting and recording career that would soon supplant his purely literary life and bring him both fame and fortune. As the following fragment from *Death of a Lady's Man* demonstrates, the younger Cohen could reach extraordinary heights of hallucinatory fancy.

The obscene silence I knelt beside a stream which was manifesting on a polished wooden floor in an apartment above Central Park. A feathered shield was fastened to my left forearm. A feathered helmet was lowered on my head. I was invested with a duty to protect the orphan and the widow. This made me feel so good I climbed on Alexandra's double bed and wept in a general way for the fate of men. Then I followed her into the bathroom. She appeared to turn gold. She stood before me as huge as the guardian of a harbour. How had I ever thought of mastering her? With a hand of chrome and an immense Gauloise cigarette she suggested that I give up and worship her, which I did for ten years. Thus began the obscene silence of my career as a lady's man.

Leonard Cohen
1978

1989

Fusions and Frictions "We used to be five families in this house, all crowded together, *tutti i familiari*, parents and kids and cousins and Nonna, and in the summertime after work everybody would be outside talking along the street.

"Now the house is quiet, quiet. On the street I hear foreigners more than our own people talking. The cousins have big places out in the suburbs now, and Dominic is gone, God rest his soul. So is my Johnny, living downtown and not with his own people.

"Angelina has done well like her father said she would, a big lawyer now. But she is so busy I hardly get to see her and the kids, and when she does call me I can't find the new telephone she bought me, the one with no cord. I curse it, and if I do find it I tell her, Angelina, Papà and I worked hard all those years so you don't have to rush home and serve your *bambini* frozen things out of that microwave flashing 12-12-12 instead of a proper clock, and she says to me, You worked too, 'a working mother,' she always calls me, and I say, You think I liked it, all those years in the hotel laundry, we worked because we had to work. And she says, Mamma, that's the other line, can I put you on hold a moment? I hang up. I know she is busy, but to put your mother on hold?

"Is this how children treat their parents in Canada, I want to say. But Dominic, he wouldn't hear a word against this country. You can get somewhere in this country, he used to say, even those first years when he worked construction and every day I worried he was going to get killed. I am Italian, he would say, but my kids, my kids are Canadians."

Canada had been attracting immigrants in large numbers since the 1950s, and not just from Europe. Immigrant cultures continued to redefine themselves, sometimes in remarkable multi-ethnic fusions, sometimes simply through generational changes.

The role of national borders changed. Brian Mulroney's business-oriented Conservatives replaced Pierre Trudeau's Liberals in Ottawa. Canada negotiated a free trade agreement with the United States. As Communism collapsed and the Berlin Wall fell at the end of the decade, a new word, "globalization," began to enter the language. Some who had adapted to a different kind of Canada were troubled by the pace of the changes.

"Dominic was so proud when Angelina won all the prizes at school and the law school after. When she had the baby, I thought, now she will stay home. But they have a little Filipina to help, and when Angie brings the family over, she says my cooking doesn't 'agree' with my son-in-law, so they don't stay. With a mangia-cake name like his, maybe it is not so crazy, Angie keeping her own name.

"My Johnny, he calls. One of the first times he came home after his father died, he brought his friend with him. My sister-in-law said Dominic would not have let them in his house. Finally I told her, it is my house now. He is a nice Italian boy, Johnny's friend, he loves *polenta pasticciata* just like I always made it. Sometimes I think he would have been perfect for my Angie! When they were leaving that first time and I told them to come back Sunday, Johnny gave me a hug, and he said, 'Welcome to the 1980s, Mamma.'"

Visions 1980–1989

1980 April Terry Fox set out from St. John's, Newfoundland, on his "Marathon of Hope," but he was forced to give up his coast-to-coast odyssey in Thunder Bay, Ontario, in September. The cancer that had caused his right leg to be amputated had spread to his lungs. But Fox's marathon raised millions of dollars for cancer research. By the time he died a year later he had become a hero to thousands. His example continues to raise money for the cancer cause through the annual Terry Fox fundraising run.

1980 July Former Canadian ambassador to Iran Kenneth Taylor was made an Officer of the Order of Canada. During the U.S. embassy hostage crisis in Tehran the year before, Taylor had pulled off the "Canadian Caper," spiriting six Americans hidden in the Canadian embassy out of Iran under false Canadian passports. This act of derring-do made Taylor an instant celebrity in the United States. He was awarded the Congressional Gold Medal by the Americans and handed the plum posting of consul general in New York by the Canadians.

1981 September Alberta Premier Peter Lougheed and Prime Minister Pierre Trudeau signed the 1981 Energy Pricing Agreement that finally gave the producing provinces a say in the price they charged for oil and gas. A few months earlier, this protester on the steps of the Alberta legislature in Edmonton had summed up Albertans' anger over federal energy policy in general and Pierre Trudeau in particular. The new deal removed one grievance from the list but did little to assuage growing Western alienation.

1981 November Prime Minister Pierre Trudeau, Finance Minister Allan MacEachen, and Quebec Premier René Lévesque at a meeting of Canadian first ministers in Ottawa (*top*). The meeting ended with a deal, brokered without Quebec's participation or consent, for bringing home the Canadian constitution. "Trudeau m'a fourré [Trudeau has fucked me]," Lévesque sobbed as he flew home. He had a point. The patriated constitution would include a protection for minority-language rights, challenging the PQ's attempt to legislate a unilingual province, a move that had alarmed Quebec Anglos (*above*).

1981 November A Hoser Day Parade in Toronto attracted 5,000 people wearing earmuffs, toques, and flannel shirts. The guests of honour were *SCTV* stars Rick Moranis and Dave Thomas, better known as Bob and Doug McKenzie (*top*). The McKenzie Brothers, who became a brief but huge North American cult phenomenon, had first appeared as a satiric response to a demand from regulators for more Canadian content. Not coincidentally, 1981 was also the year *SCTV* (whose cast is pictured above) made it on American TV – the latest successful export of Canadian comic talent in a line stretching back to Wayne and Shuster.

1981 Fall Canadian movie production was on the rise thanks to government support for home-grown cinema. Dozens of films, including *Meat the Cleaver* and *Hog Wild*, were made but never released. And the likes of Dan Aykroyd, Bill Murray, and John Candy all made their first movies in Hollywood North. Possibly the lowest-brow and definitely the highest-grossing of these 1980s Canflicks was *Porky's*, which one reviewer described as "a slapstick adolescent wet dream," about six high school chums who go to a sleazy bar in search of loose women (*above*).

1982 April Queen Elizabeth II signing the Constitution Act, 1982, beside Pierre Trudeau in Ottawa. "History will show that nothing essential to the originality of Quebec has been sacrificed," the prime minister intoned, while René Lévesque led a bitter protest in Montreal. As for Queen Elizabeth, according to Stephen Clarkson and Christina McCall, she "had the air of a disapproving Visitor presiding over a college prize-giving where the upper-form prefects were in disgrace. Her pursed mouth was said to reflect her discomfort with the fact that Quebec had been left out of the constitutional accord."

1982 October Laurie Skreslet of Calgary would become the first Canadian to stand on the summit of Mount Everest, but not before the Canadian Mount Everest Expedition (*above*) had been marked by tragedy when three Nepalese Sherpas and a Canadian climber died. Earlier in 1982, Canadians mourned another tragedy after 84 crew members, 56 of them Newfoundlanders, died when a fierce storm capsized the *Ocean Ranger*, the world's largest semisubmersible drilling rig.

1982 March Scottish-born jurist Bertha Wilson was appointed Canada's first woman Supreme Court judge. Wilson, who had gained a reputation as a smart and progressive judge on the Ontario Court of Appeal, would serve on a court suddenly empowered to interpret the new Canadian Charter of Rights and Freedoms. Among other decisions to which she contributed was the 1988 striking down of Canada's abortion law. "If women lawyers and women judges through differing perspectives on life can bring a new humanity to bear on the decision-making process," she once said, "perhaps they will make a difference." **425**

1983 July Protesters across Canada, including these two, demonstrated against the testing of U.S. cruise missiles in northern Alberta. Some compared the government's decision to allow the testing to the BOMARC missile controversy of the 1960s, when the issue was whether to mount nuclear warheads on Canadian missiles deployed as part of Canada's commitment to North American defence. In both cases the debate pointed up an essential split in the national psyche: Canadians generally approve of their military alliance with the United States but don't want to know the details.

1983 Summer Prince Charles and Princess Diana arrived in Halifax to a rapturous welcome at the beginning of Diana's first visit to Canada. Charles expressed his delight at "the opportunity to introduce my wife to a large number of Canadians." Diana outshone her older and stuffier husband throughout their Canadian tour. In Ottawa, where fans began lining up at 6 a.m. for a glimpse of the princess, they shouted, "We want Diana, we want Diana!" The stunningly dressed, radiantly smiling Diana did not disappoint. Millions of Canadians fell in love with her.

1984 February Speed skater Gaëtan Boucher (*left*) garnered two gold medals and one bronze at the Winter Olympics in Sarajevo, the best showing ever by a Canadian. Also celebrating in 1984 was John Turner (*above*), whose victory at a leadership convention in June made him Liberal leader and prime minister. But his prize was tarnished by the bouquet of controversial patronage appointments that Pierre Trudeau left his successor as a parting gift.

1984 May Wayne Gretzky (*right*) led the Edmonton Oilers to their first of three Stanley Cups, beginning an Oiler reign that ended four years later when the Great One abandoned Edmonton for the greener pastures of Los Angeles. As great in the musical sphere was jazz pianist Oscar Peterson, here acknowledging the crowd's applause at the Montreal International Jazz Festival in July (*above*). In September, throngs welcomed Pope John Paul II everywhere he went during his cross-Canada tour, including this huge congregation gathered at an airfield in Namao, Alberta, for an open-air mass (*top*).

1984 October The Inuit of northern Quebec blamed Hydro-Québec's massive James Bay power project when more than 20,000 caribou were swept over Limestone Falls while crossing the Caniapiscau River. The Inuit believed the river's waters had been swollen by the opening of dam spillways upstream. This incident was but one of many conflicts that pitted the forces of economic development against indigenous people, conservationists, and occasionally eco-terrorists. The 1980s were the decade when "going green" went mainstream.

1985 March Prime Minister Brian Mulroney (left) and Ronald Reagan met in Quebec City on St. Patrick's Day in the so-called Shamrock Summit. Behind the blarney, which peaked with the two leaders publicly crooning "When Irish Eyes Are Smiling," the summit initiated a momentous change in Canadian policy: the president and the prime minister agreed to work towards free trade between their countries. Mulroney's move was a personal about-face – he had opposed free trade during the 1984 campaign – and an abandonment of Tory orthodoxy going back to the National Policy of Sir John A. Macdonald.

1985 February The brightest lights in Canadian popular music – and quite a few lesser lights – gathered in a recording studio to lay down the vocals for "Tears Are Not Enough," a pop single to raise money for Ethiopian famine relief and Canadian food banks. Bryan Adams, the hottest star of the moment, helped pen the lyrics, and the music-industry celebs were joined by the 1985 NHL All-Star team. The song may have been forgettable, but its sales nearly broke the previous Canadian record set by Bobby Gimby's patriotic jingle "Ca-na-da," which sold 300,000 copies during the Centennial frenzy of 1967.

In addition to Adams, quite a few past and present Canadian stars joined the chorus, including Anne Murray, Corey Hart, Joni Mitchell, Oscar Peterson, Jane Siberry, Neil Young, Tommy Hunter, Sylvia Tyson, and Rompin' Ronnie Hawkins. The Canadian music scene had exploded after Canadian content regulations – CanCon – were introduced in the early 1970s, but according to the authors of the popcult classic *Mondo Canuck*, "musically speaking" the 1980s were "possibly the driest, flattest and most uninspiring stretch on the entire trans-Canadian pop highway."

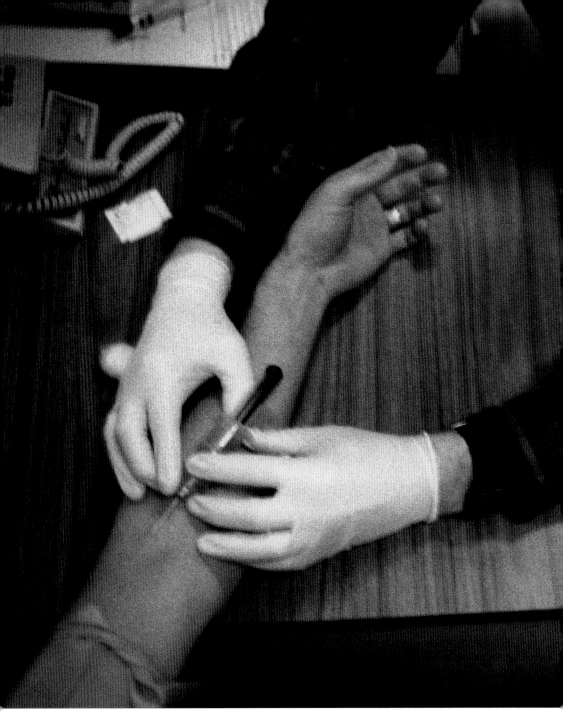

1985 Spring An anonymous volunteer providing a blood sample as part of a University of Toronto epidemiological study of Acquired Immune Deficiency Syndrome (AIDS). The study, involving volunteers who suspected they were at risk of developing AIDS, also collected behavioural data. At this stage in the history of the AIDS epidemic, the root of the syndrome – a virus that attacks and progressively destroys the body's immune system – had not yet been isolated and no effective treatment had been developed. Thus a positive diagnosis was a death warrant.

1985 Summer These carefree girls in Kitchener, Ontario, didn't know it, but by the time they grew old enough to have children of their own, the family allowance would be history. In January 1986 the Mulroney government would end the full indexing of family allowances to the cost of living, a policy change that signalled a move away from the universality of social programs. In 1992, the Conservatives would introduce the Child Tax Benefit, a non-refundable payment geared to income.

1986 May In Vancouver Expo 86 opened with a flourish, including among its 65 pavilions from 41 countries the elaborate Chinese pavilion (*above*). Bearing the theme "World in Motion – World in Touch," all the pavilions related to global transportation and communications. It was the largest special category exposition ever held. Vancouver's summer of Expo was blessed with wonderful weather, and the fair's success seemed to reinforce the sense that Canada's West Coast metropolis had truly come into its own among the cities of the world.

1987 October This photograph of a worried floor trader in Toronto only hints at the huge scale of the 1987 stock market crash, which triggered the worst recession in Canada since the Great Depression. The latest round of economic hard times helped sour the ratification process for the recently achieved Meech Lake Accord. The accord was designed to finally bring Quebec into the constitutional fold, and included "the recognition that Quebec constitutes within Canada a distinct society."

439

1988 August A member of the first Canadian contingent of the United Nations force heading to the Persian Gulf to police the ceasefire in the war between Iran and Iraq. The nearly 500 troops faced yet another peacekeeping challenge, a task in which no country had more experience or more achievements than Canada. Since Lester Pearson had helped invent the concept in 1956, Canadians had become specialists in this delicate form of military activity, serving in every corner of the globe and seldom firing a shot, except in warning.

1988 September As if Canadians weren't dealing with enough disappointment during the recession-plagued late 1980s, one of the decade's great moments of sports pride turned to shame when Ben Johnson's world-record-breaking 100-metre sprint at the Seoul Olympics (*right*) was disallowed after he tested positive for banned drugs. Even bleaker news hit the Canadian prairies as the year-long drought showed no sign of ending. Images like this scene so eerily reminiscent of the dust bowls of the Great Depression fuelled the national sense of unceasing economic malaise.

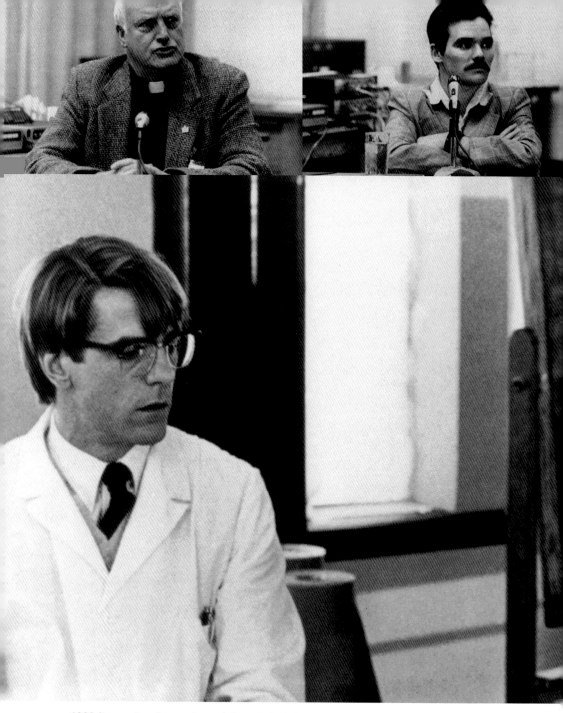

1988 September Jeremy Irons (*above*, left) being directed by David Cronenberg (*above*, right) in his creepy hit *Dead Ringers*, which opened the Toronto Festival of Festivals but was released to decidedly mixed reviews. Irons starred as identical twin gynecologists who conduct an affair with the same woman patient, played by Canadian actress Geneviève Bujold. Cronenberg's unsettling take on female sexual abuse and the dark corners of the male psyche confirmed that the nice-guy image of Canadian culture – noble Mounties set against mountain panoramas – no longer applied.

Canadians were nonetheless shocked by the revelations of child abuse at the Mount Cashel Orphanage in St. John's, Newfoundland, that came to light in 1988 and were aired in detail during a public inquiry in 1989. Among many, the inquiry heard testimony from these four men (*top, left to right*): Father Kevin Malloy, a teaching priest who had received reports of the abuse but assumed the police were handling them; John Willis, who'd made a complaint in 1975; Robert Conners, who said he'd been abused by three Christian Brothers; Shane Earle, whose abuse began the day he arrived at the orphanage.

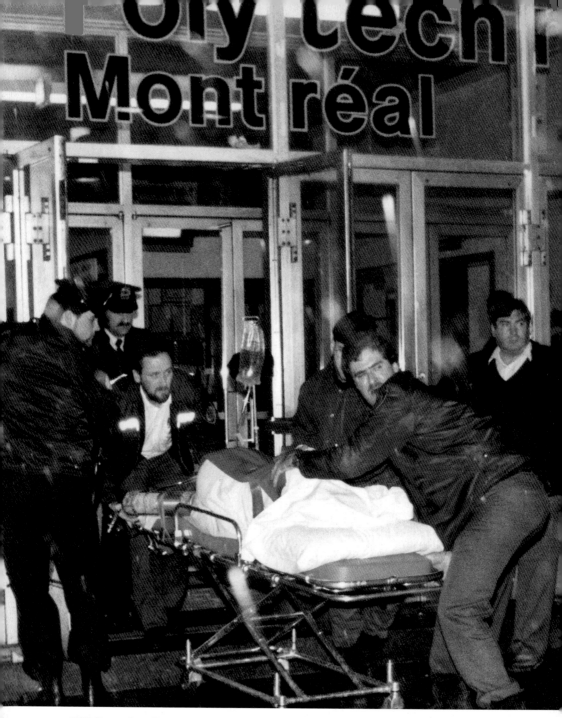

1989 December Rescue workers rushing a victim of the Montreal Massacre from the École polytechnique at the Université de Montréal. The gunman, Marc Lépine, had opened fire in an engineering classroom after separating the female students from the male. He killed fourteen women and wounded thirteen others before shooting himself. Lépine may have been crazy, but as newly elected NDP leader Audrey McLaughlin would later write, "His anger – and his need to express that anger through violence – is shared by many who are all too sane." McLaughlin was one of thousands attending the funeral (*right*).

Voices 1980–1989

"Cheap, small and powerful computers are reaching into every sector of the economy, introducing automation and change on a scale unmatched by any previous technology," wrote *Toronto Star* publisher Beland Honderich in his introduction to the fourth volume of the Walter L. Gordon Lecture Series, an annual series on Canadian themes in honour of the former finance minister and economic nationalist. In the 1979–80 series, T. R. Ide, president of Information and Communications Technology, based in Scarborough, Ontario, spoke on "Canada in the Age of Microelectronics."

Is it something alien? **As computers become smaller and cheaper, they will become more ubiquitous and will intrude more and more on our lives. As they become smarter and faster, they will take over a greater and greater share of the decisions that we are accustomed to make for ourselves or at least decisions that we are prepared to permit those we trust to make for us.**

T.R. Ide
circa 1980

But how much do we understand about the nature of the computer? Is it an extension of ourselves in the sense that tools such as hoes, shovels and bicycles are? Or is it more like the aeroplane which we utilize to do something that inherently we are unable to do?...

Is the "god in the machine" human or is it something alien? If it is human, then can it be used to enrich human relationships or will it impoverish them?

In Alice Munro's highly personal oeuvre, mostly set in the southwestern Ontario where she was born and still lives, it is sometimes difficult to discern where autobiography ends and fiction begins. In her words, her work is "autobiographical in form but not in fact." This passage is from the title story in *The Moons of Jupiter* (1982).

Middle-aged in our twenties **I remember the television programs – *Popeye the Sailor*, *The Three Stooges*, *Funorama*. When *Funorama* came on it was time to turn on the lights and cook supper. But I couldn't tell the years apart. We lived outside Vancouver in a dormitory suburb: Dormir, Dormer, Dormouse – something like that. I was sleepy all the time then; pregnancy made me sleepy, and the night feedings, and the West Coast rain falling. Dark dripping cedars, shiny dripping laurel; wives yawning, napping, visiting, drinking coffee, and folding diapers; husbands coming home at night from the city across the water. Every night I kissed my homecoming husband in his wet Burberry and hoped he might wake me up; I served up meat and potatoes and one of the four vegetables he permitted. He ate with a violent appetite, then fell asleep on the living-room sofa. We had become a cartoon couple, more middle-aged in our twenties than we would be in middle age.**

Alice Munro
1982

Signed by Queen Elizabeth II on April 17, the Constitution Act, 1982, made Canada a fully sovereign state. The document, which was the subject of intense negotiations by the federal and provincial governments, was agreed upon by all parties except the province of Quebec and includes an affirmation of the rights and freedoms of Canadian democratic society. Part I of the act lays out the fundamental freedoms conferred upon every Canadian citizen.

Guarantee of Rights and Freedoms

Constitution Act 1982

1. The *Canadian Charter of Rights and Freedoms* guarantees the rights and freedoms set out in it subject only to such reasonable limits prescribed by law as can be demonstrably justified in a free and democratic society.
2. Everyone has the following fundamental freedoms:
   (a) freedom of conscience and religion;
   (b) freedom of thought, belief, opinion and expression, including freedom of the press and other media of communication;
   (c) freedom of peaceful assembly; and
   (d) freedom of association.

By the time Ken Dryden retired from a stellar NHL career, having backstopped the Montreal Canadiens to six Stanley Cups, he had already earned a law degree and a reputation as the thinking man's hockey player. (He was nicknamed "the Thinker" for his relaxed stance at the net.) He then proved that he could write. His first book, *The Game*, remains one of the best ever examinations of professional sport from a player's point of view.

Ken Dryden 1983

And my body moves When a game gets close to me, or threatens to get close, my conscious mind goes blank. I feel nothing, I hear nothing, my eyes watch the puck, my body moves – like a goalie moves, like I move; I don't tell it to move or how to move or where, I don't know it's moving, I don't feel it move – yet it moves. And when my eyes watch the puck, I see things I don't know I'm seeing. I see Larson and Nedomansky as they come on the ice, I see them away from the puck unthreatening and uninvolved. I see something in the way a shooter holds his stick, in the way his body angles and turns, in the way he's being checked, in what he's done before that tells me what he'll do – and my body moves. I let it move. I trust it and the unconscious mind that moves it.

Jane Jacobs loves cities, and perhaps more than any thinker of the second half of the twentieth century she has helped us understand how they work – and why they don't. Her seminal *The Death and Life of Great American Cities* (1961) has profoundly influenced generations of town planners. In the following passage from *Cities and the Wealth of Nations* (1984), Jacobs argues that vibrant cities that nurture innovation are the *sine qua non* of a successful national economy.

The civilized art of maintaining creative cities

Jane Jacobs
1984

Let us fantasize a Big Experimental System in which we are all included. Information feeds back into the system, and from time to time the burden of the feedback is that such-and-such a society has allowed its cities to languish, or that in such-and-such a civilization the cities are already well down the drain. The feedback seems to operate on the premise that people who relinquish the civilized art of maintaining creative cities are not to be entrusted with the risks of developing further. This fantasy is not *entirely* metaphor. If we strip it of the judgmental word "entrusted," we are left with a hard, plain truth. Societies and civilizations in which the cities stagnate don't develop and flourish further. They deteriorate.

Michael Ondaatje's image-laden works of fiction often seem closer to poetry than to traditional narrative fiction. The following passage from *In the Skin of a Lion*, his only novel set in Canada, describes in evocatively photographic terms the building of Toronto's Bloor Street Viaduct during the 1930s.

Time-lapse evolution The bridge goes up in a dream.

Michael Ondaatje
1987

It will link the east end with the centre of the city. It will carry traffic, water, and electricity across the Don Valley. It will carry trains that have not even been invented yet.

Night and day. Fall light. Snow light. They are always working – horses and wagons and men arriving for work on the Danforth side at the far end of the valley.

There are over 4,000 photographs from various angles of the bridge in its time-lapse evolution. The piers sink into bedrock fifty feet below the surface through clay and shale and quicksand – 45,000 cubic yards of earth are evacuated. The network of scaffolding stretches up.

Men in a maze of wooden planks climb deep into the shattered light of blond wood. A man is an extension of hammer, drill, flame. Drill smoke in his hair. A cap falls into the valley, gloves buried in stone dust.

Love him or hate him, no one can deny that Brian Mulroney changed Canada in fundamental ways. Certainly his most lasting and far-reaching legacy is the North American Free Trade Agreement, which Canadian nationalists denounced as the beginning of the end of Canada as an independent country. One of the most frequent criticisms made of Mulroney as prime minister was that he was far too cozy with the Americans. In a speech to the House of Commons in September 1988, he addressed that criticism head on.

A uniquely Canadian way of life
We are proud of our distinctiveness as Canadians, of the values that mark us clearly as Canadians. We are determined to preserve and enrich those qualities, which ensure a uniquely Canadian way of life. Our future will be built by Canadians doing their very best, by Canadians providing world-class results, and a genuine national commitment to excellence.

Mr. Speaker, those born in Canada and those who have chosen it for its [*sic*] home, may share in this great enterprise. Let's give them the chance to get on with the job. The decision is for all of us. Canadians have the fundamental ability to compete and excel. As a government, our responsibility is to provide the best environment possible to allow Canadians, individual Canadians, with their chance to succeed. I believe, Mr. Speaker, we can do this by endorsing the free trade agreement today. By doing so, we say yes to free trade, yes to jobs for our youth, yes to a more prosperous future for Canada.

Brian Mulroney
1988

On August 9, 1988, the news broke that the Edmonton Oilers had traded Wayne Gretzky to the Los Angeles Kings. (The deal had actually been agreed to two weeks earlier, but only on the condition that the official announcement be withheld until the Oilers' season ticket drive had ended.) According to Peter Pocklington, the financially strapped team owner, Gretzky and his new American wife, the actress Janet Jones, had requested the deal. Said Pocklington, "Anyone involved in a committed relationship knows that changes are brought by marriage. I truly understood when Wayne approached me and asked to be traded to the Los Angeles Kings." But at a press conference he called two weeks later, on August 22, Gretzky told a somewhat different version of the story.

Pleasing people
"I wasn't going to let anyone tell me where I would be playing. I'd made that decision. I've been pleasing people all my life, so now I decide to do what's best for Wayne Gretzky. I would've liked to finish my career in Edmonton...I offered to sign an eight-year contract. All they had to do was agree to a no-trade clause. They wouldn't do it."

Wayne Gretzky
1988

June Callwood's concern for people with AIDS led her, in the late 1980s, to found Toronto's Casey House, a hospice for terminally ill AIDS patients. The hospice was named after her son Casey, who had died in a tragic accident. In her 1988 book *Jim: A Life with AIDS*, she tells the story of Toronto actor Jim St. James, who was an early resident of Casey House.

Enough to kill him

June Callwood
1988

He looked in the mirror and felt sympathy for the person he saw. That person in the reflection had a sad life. He was sick with a terrible disease and he had never found his love.

Jim laid out the clothes he wanted to be wearing in his coffin. On the coffee table, where no one could miss them, he put the farewell letters he had written to friends and family and the tape he wanted played at his funeral.

He showered, shaved, and put on cologne. He slipped into a clean jogging suit that he wears as pyjamas. He opened his medicine cabinet and took out an almost full bottle of Halcyon sleeping pills. They wouldn't be enough to kill him, he decided. They would need help to stop his lungs and heart. He found some Tylenol 3s, a codeine prescription given him for pain. That would do it.

On December 6, 1989, a young man named Marc Lépine murdered 14 women at the École polytechnique of the Université de Montréal. In a suicide note found on Lépine's body, he had written, "I have decided to send Ad Patres [to the fathers] the feminists who have ruined my life." Of the many expressions of shock and outrage from both men and women, journalist Stevie Cameron's award-winning essay "Our Daughters, Ourselves" was one of the most telling.

Our bright and shining daughters

Stevie Cameron
1989

Now our daughters have been shocked to the core, as we all have, by the violence in Montreal. They hear the women were separated from the men and meticulously slaughtered by a man who blamed his troubles on feminists. They ask themselves why nobody was able to help the terrified women, to somehow stop the hunter as he roamed the engineering building.

So now our daughters are truly frightened and it makes their mothers furious that they are frightened. They survived all the childhood dangers, they were careful as we trained them to be, they worked hard. Anything was possible and our daughters proved it. And now they are more scared than they were when they were little girls.

Fourteen of our bright and shining daughters won places in engineering schools, doing things we, their mothers, only dreamed of. That we lost them has broken our hearts; what is worse, is that we are not surprised.

Nearing a New Millennium

Subject: Re: digital panic

Date: Fri, 31 Dec 1999 23:59:59 PST

At 00:00 31/12/99, you wrote:
>We are wrapping a story on linkages between the Y2K
>crisis, millennial anxiety, and your leader's phrase,
>constitutional panic. Any background you can offer?

Panic has been good business the whole decade.

Our startup, back when, was a corporate client in panic mode. Their VP Information Services had mastered the double-click and thought he was Bill Gates. Pointed out to him that he had signed off on acquisition of 286 clones for the whole infrastructure. Whoa, digital panic!

There's always business in terrifying some bandwidth-challenged middle management guy. Firewalls against hackers and spammers, that was good. Push technology had them in sweat mode for a while. When the Yanks sub-poenaed Microsoft's email traffic in that web-browser thing, I did lots of speaks on email retention strategy.

But for digital panic, there never was anything like Y2K. No one could find enough code pushers. We outsourced in gigaloads, and the billables were still mega. Y2K turned us all into sleep camels. Store up a three-day weekend, pretty much hack it straight through the workweek. Heavy traffic down the carpal tunnel expressway! We put in one of those designer-coffee wagons. Amazing how far you can fly a coder squadron in Starbucks overdrive.

Just when every last IS division finally hardwired the

concept that "Y2K bug" doesn't mean the new VW Beetle, we got our takeover offer by some Silicon Valley server-farm corp looking to diversify. They paid in stock options, but when they did their IPO, I cashed out big time. Hell, the babe at the coffee wagon cashed out big time.

So I was rich and semi-retired, and looking for a concept to build a tax shelter around, you know. The environment seems so yesterday. Then this cowboy client in Calgary, very cutting-edge, split with Preston Manning over that alternative thing. He got me thinking about political applications of our technology apps.

We threw research at it, downloaded a lot of source code on voting and the Constitution, took a sat-feed of the CPAC channel. And it all seemed so British North America, man, retro. Meech, Charlottetown, Lucien Bouchard…The country couldn't sort signal out of the noise.

I knew that mode. Constitution panic is just a delta shift on the digital version. I told my Calgary cowboy we were in business. We started to conceptualize democracy in the electronic environment. I mean, those dudes in the House of Commons, I don't think so, we are all wired now. Marking an X on a ballot in the school gym? Don't even think about going there.

Our Digital Frontier Concept, www.dfc.ca, is beta-testing an Electronic Senate. The next leadership convention will have to be digital, networked, and online. With virtual politics, my cowboy could acquire the whole government franchise, hostile takeover. The correlations look strong.

Twenty-first century belongs to e-Canada. Don't panic, man.

Visions 1990–1999

1990 February Kimiko Okano Murakami at home on Saltspring Island, British Columbia. Murakami's family lost everything during World War II when they were interned and their property confiscated, yet "in her conversations, there is never a hint of her sufferings," wrote her daughter, "or of the sacrifices she made for the family's survival. Instead, when in her presence one feels the aura of strength that enabled her to succeed in life." As the century entered its final decade, many Canadians turned to their elders for a sense of connectedness to a past receding unimaginably fast. **459**

These Lands are under The native sovereignty
of The Mohawk People of Kanesatake
so respect The natural beauty of The
Land for The future generation
PLATTSBURGH
MARINA
WIND RIVER

1990 June New Democratic Party MLA Elijah Harper raising his fist in victory (*left*) on the steps of the Manitoba legislature after refusing to provide the unanimous consent necessary for Manitoba's ratification of the Meech Lake Accord, which subsequently died. Harper's act of aboriginal protest was mild compared with events a few weeks later. Near Oka, Quebec, a police officer was killed during an attack on a blockade set up by Mohawk Warriors, among them the masked gunman (*above*), from the Kanesatake Reserve. The standoff ended peacefully after Canadian troops (*top*) were called in.

1991 May The RCMP's decision to allow Sikh officers to wear turbans offended many. The first turbaned graduate was Constable Baltej Singh Dhillon, here standing with his classmates at the force's Regina training centre. Diane Francis writing in the *Financial Post* had this to say on the subject: "To me, allowing a mounted policeman to wear a turban is equivalent to letting someone change the words to our anthem or fly our flag with a fleur-de-lis or stars-and-stripes in the corner."

1991 September Joyce Milgaard demanding that Prime Minister Brian Mulroney order a review of her son David's murder conviction. Mulroney mouthed encouraging words. It was good politics but bad form – at least in the eyes of Justice Minister Kim Campbell, who'd been wrestling with whether to order the judicial review the Milgaards wanted. "The PM had blindsided me on one of my most difficult issues," Campbell wrote in her memoirs. (In the end Campbell did order a review, which led to Milgaard's release. DNA analysis subsequently confirmed his innocence.)

1992 January Roberta Bondar (*above*) became the first Canadian woman in space when she blasted off aboard the space shuttle *Discovery*. During her eight days in orbit, Bondar, a former professor of neurology, conducted experiments aimed at learning ways to extend human endurance in space. Also flying high in 1992 were the Toronto Blue Jays, who in October defeated the Atlanta Braves, four games to three, to win the World Series. Here outfielder Joe Carter is being mobbed by teammates after making the final out of the final game in Atlanta.

1993 February Sue Rodriguez preparing for another day in court. In 1991 Rodriguez had been diagnosed with amyotrophic lateral sclerosis, popularly called Lou Gehrig's disease, a condition that leads to progressive muscle atrophy, complete paralysis, and finally death. She went to court to get legal sanction for physician-assisted suicide. The Supreme Court of Canada turned her down, but her crusade for the right to die with dignity brought the debate about euthanasia into the mainstream. On the ides of March 1994 she died of an overdose of morphine combined with Seconal capsules.

1993 January Karla Homolka, here leaving the family home in St. Catharines, Ontario, with her younger sister Lori, went on trial for manslaughter in the deaths of Kristen French and Leslie Mahaffy. The manslaughter charge was the result of a plea bargain in exchange for her testimony against her husband, Paul Bernardo. Bernardo's trial in 1995 lasted four months and resulted in his conviction on all nine charges, including two counts of murder. Bernardo was declared a dangerous offender, ineligible for parole. Homolka's twelve-year sentence meant she could walk out of prison as early as mid-2001.

1993 April Premier Mike Harcourt of British Columbia announced that his government would allow logging at Clayoquot Sound, an area that included the last major stand of old-growth timber on Vancouver Island. While Harcourt promised to preserve about one-third of the Clayoquot forest, environmentalists, among them renowned wildlife artist Robert Bateman, were outraged, arguing that the remaining ancient Pacific rainforest was a treasure of spiritual as well as ecological importance. Bateman once compared a clearcut landscape seen from the air to "the shaved head of a concentration camp victim."

1993 June A convention in Ottawa elected Kim Campbell leader of the Progressive Conservatives, making her Canada's first woman prime minister. Campbell's sudden rise was assisted by this July 1990 Barbara Woodley photo, which went largely unnoticed until late 1992, when an exhibition of Woodley's portraits of women opened in Ottawa. The next day the *Ottawa Citizen* put Campbell on the front page above the caption "Doing justice to art." Campbell's image of freshness and unconventionality soon soured, and her disastrous fall election campaign left the once mighty Tories with only two seats.

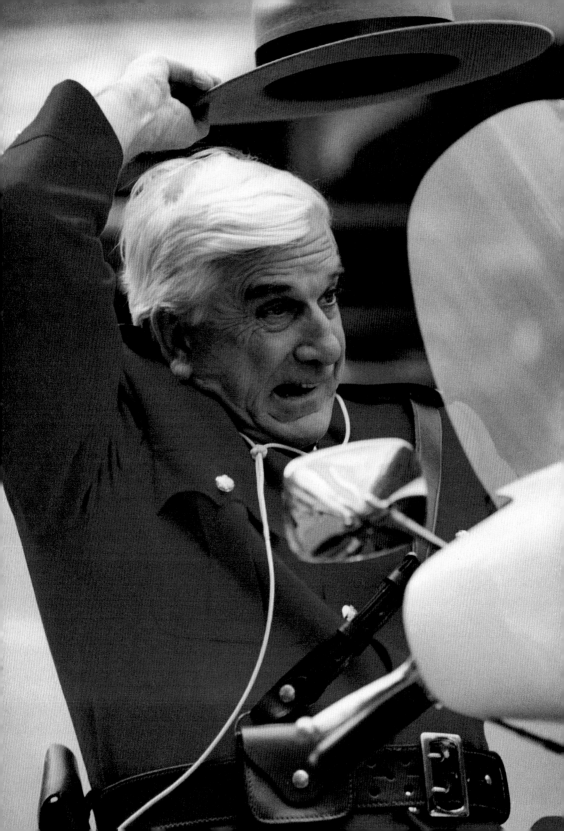

1995 March The Royal Canadian Mounted Police sold merchandising rights to the Mountie insignia and image to the Disney Corporation, marking the ultimate Hollywoodization of Canada's most recognizable figure. In Hollywood North, a new Mountie joined the force when Sergeant Duncan "Buck" Frobisher – a.k.a. Canadian actor Leslie Nielsen (*left*) – guest-starred on the popular television show *Due South*. Other 1990s Cancult exports of note included the Gen-X comedy troupe Kids in the Hall (*above*, in a still from *Brain Candy*), *Baywatch* babe Pamela Anderson Lee (*top left*), and music megastar Céline Dion (*top right*). **471**

1995 July Teens crowding in front of the stage in the Lollapalooza rock festival mosh pit (*above*). One mosher described the activity as "a ritual frenzied dance that combines the thrill of agony with the warmth of community." No such demonstrations of joy marked the No side's razor-thin victory in October in the latest referendum on Quebec sovereignty. The only real winner was Bloc Québécois leader Lucien Bouchard, whose messianic rhetoric and skilful appeal to Québécois feelings of collective grievance made him the Parti Québécois heir apparent despite the defeat of the campaign he had led.

1996 February Was Prime Minister Jean Chrétien showing his true colours when he strong-armed protester Bill Clennett (*top, far left to far right*) at a Flag Day fest in Hull, Quebec? The PM, who likes to be seen as an unvarnished man of the people, was unapologetic. "Something happened to somebody who should not have been there," he opaquely remarked. The incident soon entered popular discourse as Chrétien's "Shawinigan handshake." Another controversial fistic feat involved Danielle House, Miss Canada (*above*), here signing an autograph during a Santa Claus parade in St. John's.

Danielle House, the former Miss Newfoundland, lost her Miss Canada crown after "she bopped the new girlfriend of her old boyfriend," to quote the *Globe and Mail*, at a bar in the Newfoundland capital. Gentler means of persuasion were adopted by Craig Kielburger (*above*), a thirteen-year-old from Thornhill, Ontario, who upstaged the 1996 Team Canada trade mission to India by highlighting the obscenity of child labour. "No country has ever eliminated child labour without providing compulsory education for all," he argued.

1996 Summer Sprinter Donovan Bailey helped salve the shame of the Ben Johnson scandal when he broke the world record for 100 metres at the Atlanta Olympics (*above*), then picked up a second gold medal running anchor for the Canadian relay team. At the same games, rower Silken Laumann, here resting on her shell after the race (*opposite, top left*), won a silver in the singles sculls. But Laumann's bronze at Barcelona in 1992 shone more brightly for many, having been earned even though she had broken her ankle during a training accident just before the event.

The year 1996 was good for Canadian athletes. Elvis Stojko (*top right*) won the World Figure Skating Championships in Lausanne, Switzerland, inheriting the mantle most recently worn by Kurt Browning. And Jacques Villeneuve, here kissing his girlfriend after posting the best time in the British Grand Prix (*above*), won the Formula One racing championship after coming first in seven Grand Prix races. His late father, Gilles, would have been proud.

1996 November Native Korean War veteran Leon Fontaine (standing) and national chief of the Assembly of First Nations Ovide Mercredi at the National War Memorial during Remembrance Day ceremonies in Ottawa. During Mercredi's controversial tenure as national chief he showed considerable talent for drawing attention to First Nations rights and grievances, but was accused of failing to consult his membership regularly before taking action. In 1997 he would be replaced by rival Manitoba chief Phil Fontaine.

1997 July The Somalia Inquiry released its report into the torture and killing of Somali civilian Shidane Arone by members of the Canadian Airborne Regiment during the Canadian peacekeeping mission to the Horn of Africa in 1993. The inquiry had widened to become an investigation of the whole Canadian military system after the 1995 broadcast of videotapes showing the Airborne's drunken and grotesque hazing rituals, which included harnessing a black soldier and walking him like a dog. *Above*: A grab from one of the hazing videos.

1997 May Peter Gzowski taped his last episode of *Morningside* in Moose Jaw, Saskatchewan, bringing to an end the remarkable radio show that had been on air since September 1982. *Globe and Mail* cultural critic Bronwyn Drainie called *Morningside* "a Canadian cultural miracle." Gzowski once referred to the show as "a sort of village bulletin board for the nation." During its three hours of broadcast each weekday morning, it offered interviews with the famous and the obscure, readings of wonderful and literate letters from listeners, slices of radio drama, and Canadian musical intermezzi.

Many Canadians believed that *Morningside* knitted people and regions together like no other program on radio or television. In its final years it claimed a remarkable 15 percent of the radio audience, a testament to Gzowski's disarming manner and to the eclectic mix of guests and topics. The elegiac photograph above was taken during one of the last tapings in the *Morningside* studio at CBC headquarters in Toronto.

1997 June The loudest political report of the 1990s was sounded by the Reform Party, which parlayed Western alienation and neo-conservative ideology into an electoral force to be reckoned with. Party leader Preston Manning, here addressing a press conference following his party's accession to official opposition status after the June election, had his eyes trained on the prime minister's job. But his colleagues occasionally showed a knack for shooting themselves in the foot. One who consistently performed well in the House and on the hustings was Edmonton MP Deborah Grey (*top*, with a .44 Magnum).

1997 May Two young women celebrating the recent decision by the Ontario Court of Appeal that overturned the 1992 conviction of Gwen Jacob for committing an indecent act. Jacob, then a 19-year-old Guelph University student, had been arrested after walking topless around downtown Guelph on a hot summer day in 1991. As a result of the court's decision, several Ontario cities permitted women to go topless in certain public places, primarily beaches and swimming pools.

1997 April–May These two scenes from the Manitoba flood (*top*) eerily resemble pictures of the 1950 inundation. Nearly 9,000 Canadian troops lent a hand, helping repair a reputation damaged by the Somalia debacle. Nothing, however, was going to fix the ruined image of Bre-X after the mining company's chief geologist, Michael de Guzman, here being mourned following his March suicide (*above*), was revealed to have faked mineral assays from the company's gold find in Borneo. *Right*: A verifiable resource came on line when this 600,000-tonne drilling rig began tapping the rich Hibernia oilfield off Newfoundland.

1997 November For their official photograph at the end of their economic summit in Vancouver, Asia-Pacific leaders gathered on the University of British Columbia campus were all smiles. But their sense of serenity had been purchased at some cost to civil liberties. In a sequence of events still causing controversy, the Prime Minister's Office apparently instructed the RCMP to deal harshly with protesters whose particular target was the repressive regime of Indonesia's president Suharto (fourth from left).

The police kept demonstrators behind a security fence. When some charged the fence, the police used pepper spray (being wiped from the eyes of the demonstrator above) and many were detained. Craig Jones, a UBC law student arrested that day, was outraged: "There was no other reason for the involvement of the prime minister's office, the department of foreign affairs, the senior level RCMP officers and the Indonesian government; there is no other purpose for their involvement here except to limit, and where possible suspend, the Constitutional rights of Canadian citizens."

1998 January The worst ice storm in memory paralyzed eastern Ontario and Quebec, leaving hundreds of thousands without power for days or even weeks and causing millions of dollars of damage to buildings and landscapes (*left*). Property was easier to repair than the damaged reputation of former hockey mogul Alan Eagleson (*top*, middle), here leaving U.S. District Court in Boston after pleading guilty to fraud. Irreparable were the broken lives of the surviving Dionne quintuplets, Annette, Yvonne, and Cecile (*above*), who in March received long-overdue compensation from the Ontario government.

1998 September South African President Nelson Mandela being helped over a step by Prime Minister Chrétien following a speech to a joint session of Parliament.

1998 November Pierre Elliott Trudeau and his former wife, Margaret, at the memorial service of their son Michel, who drowned after being swept into a mountain lake by an avalanche in British Columbia.

1999 Winter This photograph of a squeegee kid resting on a Toronto stoop attests to the more aggressive face of poverty in Canada at the end of the century. Although the economy was on the upswing and unemployment dropping, the Toronto Disaster Relief Committee could declare homelessness "a national disaster." Ironically it was the 1998 ice storm, which left hundreds of thousands temporarily homeless, that helped crystallize the problem for Toronto street nurse Cathy Crowe. "I realized that the images on television that had moved me were the daily circumstances of homeless people themselves," she wrote.

1999 March A worker putting the finishing touches on an igloo being built as part of the celebrations to mark the creation of the new territory of Nunavut. Nunavut's territorial status became official on April 1, ushering into existence the country's only political unit inhabited mostly by First Nations people. Barely 27,000 people, 85 percent of them Inuit, live in Nunavut, which comprises almost two-thirds of the former Northwest Territories.

1999 March The Serbs in this Belgrade demonstration were protesting the Canadian government's decision to join the NATO bombing campaign aimed at stopping ethnic cleansing in the Yugoslav province of Kosovo. External Affairs Minister Lloyd Axworthy justified Canada's participation as necessary to "right the wrongs that have taken place so tragically in that area in the last year or two." Canada had never before attacked a sovereign country that had not previously attacked Canada or one of its allies.

1999 June Open expressions of gay pride, virtually unthinkable even fifteen years earlier, were everywhere during Toronto's annual Gay Pride Parade, one of a series of such events held in towns and cities across the country. The Toronto extravaganza attracted an estimated 750,000 people. Major corporations from Molson's to Air Canada vied for sponsorship space, mainstream politicians jostled for media exposure, and not a few of the revellers just plain exposed themselves. But what had once seemed threatening to many Canadians now seemed harmless fun.

Whether or not the 20th century belonged to Canada, the last hundred years have seen the transformation of a fragile federation of British colonies into a sophisticated nation-state. Far out of proportion to its economic clout or military might, Canada has made a mark on the world stage. Its diplomats helped teach more combative countries the power of compromise while its writers spread the word that the "True North strong and free" came as advertised.

One wonders what Sir Wilfrid Laurier, were the great man alive today, would predict for Canada in the 21st century. But if asked to look back on the century past, he would undoubtedly be pleased with the progress of the country he helped bring to maturity.

Voices 1990–1999

The Meech Lake Accord was perceived by its originators as a means of bringing Quebec back into the "constitutional family." However, its explicit description of Canada as a country born of "two founding nations" completely ignored First Nations people. On June 15, 1990, one week before the deal finally expired, Manitoba New Democratic Party MLA Elijah Harper promised the Assembly of Manitoba Chiefs that he would fight to prevent its ratification.

The right decision I love this country, too. That's why I've said we shared this land with other people. But the strength that I got was from all of you, and also from all the elders, the prayers that have been placed to our Creator. And I believe he has answered and heard our prayer. Last night I phoned home, and I spoke to my dad. And he assured me to continue the fight. And the elders at home have been building fires in the evenings and praying for us – not only for me but for the leaders, so that they may make the right decision. And I believe we have made that decision, the right decision, but we still have to go through a few more days. And I can assure you there is support to kill the Meech Lake Accord.

Elijah Harper
1990

In May 1991, when Preston Manning gave the speech excerpted below, the Reform Party still looked to most observers like the latest in a long line of Western protest movements that had never succeeded in outgrowing their prairie populist base. As the 1993 election would prove, Reform and its leader were about to become a national force to be reckoned with.

We define a New Canada Canada's mission in the 21st century will be to create by evolution, not revolution, a more balanced society on the northern half of the North American continent...

Preston Manning
1991

New Canada must be a balanced federation, not an unbalanced federation where one province has special status or a special deal; not an unbalanced federation where all the provinces have special status and Canada has no status; not an unbalanced federation where one generation centralizes all the power in Ottawa, and the next generation centralizes it all in the provincial capitals in the name of decentralization...

New Canada must be a truly democratic federation, not a federation where powerful interest groups on the left or the right succeed in getting their ideology entrenched in the Constitution so that the public cannot choose a different course even if they want to...

Can we define a New Canada to replace the Old Canada that is dying?

Douglas Coupland didn't invent the term Generation X, but the 1991 publication of his novel of that name gave it widespread currency. Generation X became a buzzword to describe late baby-boomers who had missed the postwar prosperity and found themselves in a world of diminished expectations. The following passage from *Generation X* is typical of the ironic voice that permeates the book.

What seems to be the future **Fifteen years ago, on what remains as possibly the most unhip day of my life, my entire family, all nine of us, went to have our group portrait taken at a local photo salon. As a result of that hot and endless sitting, the nine of us spent the next fifteen years trying bravely to live up to the corn-fed optimism, the cheerful waves of shampoo, and the air-brushed teeth-beams that the resultant photo is still capable of emitting to this day. We may look dated in this photo, but we look *perfect*, too. In it, we're beaming earnestly to the right, off toward what seems to be the future but which was actually Mr. Leonard, the photographer and a lonely old widower with hair implants, holding something mysterious in his left hand and yelling, *"Fromage!"***

Douglas Coupland
1991

The fiction of Carol Shields often explores the extraordinary aspects of ordinary lives. The following passage is from *The Stone Diaries*, for which Shields, an American by birth, won both the Governor General's Award and the Pulitzer Prize. *The Stone Diaries* is the fictional autobiography of Daisy Goodwill, from her birth in 1905 until her death in the 1980s, a life that Daisy herself describes as an "assemblage of dark voids and unbridgeable gaps." The novel exists in the shadow world between fact and fiction: Shields includes photographs of Daisy's family but none of Daisy herself. The narrator remains elusive, a little like the century itself.

The past is never past **"This mean old sentimental century. It smothered her. Like a curtain. The kind you can't see through."**

Carol Shields
1993

> **"She could have divorced Dad."**
> **"For starters."**
> **"What? What are you talking about?"**
> **"Why would you think that? I mean, the two of them were reasonably happy together, all things considered."**
> **"You honestly think so?"**
> **"Well, as happy as most."**
> **"Whatever happy means."**
> **"Tell me about it."**
> **"All I know is, the past is never past."**
> **"Is that supposed to be profound?"**
> **"Hmmmmm."**

An East Indian born and raised in Trinidad, Neil Bissoondath first published fiction with themes of alienation and exile but gained prominence in 1994 with his non-fiction polemic, *Selling Illusions: The Cult of Multiculturalism in Canada*. Examining the effects of Canada's official policy of multiculturalism, Bissoondath argues that emphasizing the differences among Canadians only nurtures a sense of entitlement and separateness while doing little or nothing to increase the sense of belonging that immigrants crave.

Hyphenated Canadian citizenship Citizenship, whether through birth or naturalization, implies belonging. It implies a basic commitment of intellectual and emotional loyalty. It is a thing of value. And yet, in recent years, the diminishing value of Canadian citizenship – the creation of the hyphenated Canadian with divided loyalties, the perception that immigration policy now permits the rich to buy their way into the country, the idea that citizenship is a matter of rights and not of obligations – means that the opposite has also come to be true. Canadian citizenship is frequently seen not as a means of committing oneself to the country but simply as a way of abandoning it with an assurance of safety.

Neil Bissoondath
1994

As leader of the federal Bloc Québécois, Lucien Bouchard initially took second place to Parti Québécois premier Jacques Parizeau during the October 1995 referendum campaign on Quebec independence. But with three weeks to go, and the Yes side trailing, Bouchard took the lead, singlehandedly transforming a cakewalk for the federalist side into a cliffhanger. In this excerpt from a speech the week before the vote, Bouchard brought both passion and intellect to his cause.

Tough words The man who asks us tonight for another blank cheque on our future is the same one who benefited from our weakness, the day after the No of 1980, to rip up the Constitution of our ancestors and imposed upon us another that reduced Quebec's powers in the areas of language and education. It's this Constitution that seeks to melt our identity within the Canadian whole. How do you describe Mr. Chrétien's attitude when he says to us now that if we give him a second No, if we strip ourselves of all political strength, if we give up our solidarity, that he will not modify the Constitution without Quebec's agreement?

Lucien Bouchard
1995

Tough words come to our lips. We won't utter them; but... we won't be fools. The violated promises of 1980 and the odious blow in 1982 are too fresh in our memories...We won't let you get the best of René Lévesque. We won't deny again the "master in our own house" of Jean Lesage. We won't repudiate the beautiful slogan "equality or independence" of Daniel Johnson Sr.

Few of the CBC's annual Massey Lectures have created the stir that
accompanied the 1995 series delivered by John Ralston Saul. Saul
explored the sorry plight of the individual within the power structures
of a modern civilization, which he argues is in the thrall of a global
ideology called corporatism. This passage is from the opening chapter of
The Unconscious Civilization, the best-selling book based on his lectures.

A narrow and superficial deformation The idea of individualism, dominant today, represents a narrow and superficial deformation of the Western idea. A hijacking of the term and – since it is a central term – a hijacking of Western civilization...

John Ralston Saul
1995

The end result will be the portrait of a society addicted to
ideologies – a civilization tightly held at this moment in the
embrace of a dominant ideology: corporatism. The acceptance
of corporatism causes us to deny and undermine the legitimacy
of the individual as a citizen in a democracy. The result of such
denial is a growing imbalance which leads to our adoration
of self-interest and our denial of the public good. Corporatism
is an ideology which claims rationality as its central quality.
The overall effects on the individual are passivity and conformity
in those areas which matter and non-conformism in those
which don't.

Newfoundland comic and satirist Rick Mercer made a name for himself
on the hit CBC Television show *This Hour Has Twenty-Two Minutes*,
where he and his colleagues skewer every Canadian sacred cow they can
find. In *Streeters*, his 1996 collection of comic monologues, Mercer gave
a satiric twist to the issue of homelessness in a piece entitled "Careers."

A career choice If you walk around any city in this country you'll get hit up for loose change. And now all across Canada, towns are following the city of Ottawa's lead. Because in Ottawa they've made it illegal to ask for money!

Rick Mercer
1996

Ottawanians are very practical, and they realize that people
are homeless because they made a career choice. They went to
career day, came home, and said, "Mom, forget the BA in poli-sci
at Carleton, I'm gonna be homeless."

Being homeless pays three dollars a day, you get beaten up
a lot, and you have nowhere to sleep at night. But now you can't
do it anymore. So if you're homeless in Ottawa, you have two
choices. Become a lobbyist or stay homeless. Which means you're
not only miserable, you're also a criminal because you ask
people for money...

They say you can't legislate against stupidity. Well, now
I know why: because our legislators would be the ones doing all
the hard time – just like the homeless.

The terrible ice storm of January 1998 that ravaged eastern Ontario and southern Quebec ranked with the worst disasters of Canada's century. In "Notes from the Heart of Darkness," which appeared in *Chatelaine* that April, Quebec-based journalist Trish Snyder chronicled her family's experience of the ice and its aftermath in St-Athanase, Quebec. Here she describes day two of the storm.

We have been damaged
Everything is caked with ice. Branches look like they're draped in diamonds. It is beautiful, pristine, but also scary. Trees are hunched under the weight of the ice and foot-long icicles dangle from the roof...I'm starting to feel powerless. I think about how grimy I feel without a shower; wonder how we'll get cash when ours runs out, with most bank machines dead. I think about how I can't wash our clothes, let alone clean the house, and there doesn't seem to be an end in sight...There are few batteries or flashlights. Luckily, we'd stocked our yard with logs last October...When we take stock, we realize we've been lucky. Aside from shoes ruined in the flood and spoiled food, not much has been damaged. But in some ways I think we have been damaged – bruised in our trust of the institutions and services that we'd taken for granted. I'd always believed if disaster ever struck, measures would be in place to protect us. But when things got tough, we were pretty much on our own. It's scary on the one hand, but comforting to know that we can survive something like this.

Trish Snyder
1998

André Alexis's first novel, *Childhood*, maps the strangely deadpan life of narrator Thomas MacMillan through an intricate process involving the appraisal and reappraisal of seemingly innocent biographical details. In the following passage, Thomas provides an elegy for his youth that also serves as a sort of epitaph for the final decade of Canada's century.

Crest to crest
Time passed as it usually does, not moment to moment but crest to crest.

From 1979 to 1990, things happened around me more than they did to me: Quebec squirmed and stayed, the Constitution was signed on a windy day when I was home feverish, Clark and Turner made wonderful prime ministers, Meech Lake died, Charlottetown died; ethnic cleansing, the preservation of democracy, fatwa and jihad...so many interesting ways to say death, and then Death itself: buses fell from mountains, trains from bridges, planes from the air...

All of this I learned first from the *Citizen*, my necessary, distracting window on the world outside.

There was more, of course. There were Ilya Prigogine, Kenichi Fukui, and John Polanyi; Subrahmanyan Chandrasekhar, Carlo Rubbia, and Simon van der Meer...

I fell in love, I think, and out again.

André Alexis
1998

Photo Sources Every effort has been made to contact copyright holders. In the event of omission or error, the editor should be notified at Otherwise Inc., 356A Queen Street West, Toronto, Canada M5V 2A2.

Some agency and archive names have been abbreviated in this source list:

AGO: Art Gallery of Ontario
ANQ: Archives Nationales du Québec
BI: Beaton Institute
CBC: CBC Archives
CLA: City of Lethbridge Archives
CMCP: Canadian Museum of Contemporary Photography
CP: CP Picture Archive
CTA: City of Toronto Archives
CTA JC: City of Toronto Archives, James Collection
CVA: City of Vancouver Archives
EA: Eatons Archives (F229, Archives of Ontario)
GA: Glenbow Archives
HBCA: Hudson's Bay Company Archives
HHF: Hockey Hall of Fame
NAC: National Archives of Canada
NAC/DND: National Archives of Canada/Department of National Defence
NBC: National Ballet of Canada
NFB: National Film Board of Canada
NFPL: Niagara Falls Public Library
OA: Archives of Ontario
OH: Ontario Hydro
NSM: Nova Scotia Museum
PAA: Provincial Archives of Alberta
PABC: Provincial Archives of British Columbia
PAM: Provincial Archives of Manitoba
PANB: Provincial Archives of New Brunswick
PANL: Provincial Archives of Newfoundland
RAWF: Royal Agricultural Winter Fair Archives
SA: Saskatchewan Archives Board
SHF: Sports Hall of Fame
TRL: Toronto Reference Library
USA: University of Saskatchewan Archives
VPL: Vancouver Public Library
WM: Whyte Museum of the Canadian Archives
WS: Wilson Studio
YA: Yukon Archives
YU/TC: York University/Telegram Collection

All photos: Clockwise from top left.

Cover, front matter and back matter *Front cover:* CVA, CP, WM, CMCP; *spine:* NAC, EA; *back cover:* CP, EA, Bryce Duffy, OA; *front matter:* p.i NAC; p.v CMCP; p.vi CMCP; *back matter:* p.512 NAC.

1900–1909 p.27 NAC PA-B4588; p.28-29 NAC C6106; p.30 NAC C10454, NAC C24630; p.31 NAC C24619; p.32 TRL; p.33 NSM; p.34 NFPL; p.35 NAC C14078; p.36 CTA; p.37 CVA 2-99; p.38 NAC, NAC, NAC C16460; p.39 GA PA-58-104d, NAC, CVA 102.25; p.40-41 NAC PA-38301, NAC PA-53548, GA NA-663-1; p.42 SHF; p.43 PANB/Men 231; p.44 GA; p.45 CVA; p.46 NAC; p.47 OA S-8973; p.48-49 OA 2475 S7681, OA 2475 S7609, OA 2476 S7627; p.50 NAC PA-112013; p.51 NAC C5093; p.52-53 PABC 51747; p.54 OH; p.55 GA NA-921-18, NAC C28214, OH; p.56 NAC PA-108751; p.57 NAC C9766; p.58 PA-11616; p.59 NAC C12035; p.60-61 PABC 67870, NAC PA-38662; p.62 SHF, TRL, SHF; p.63 SHF; p.64 PANB/Men 231; p.65 CTA 4559, NAC PA-60831.

1910–1919 p.77 YA; p.78 CTA 10343; p.79 PAM N-1828; p.80-81 CTA JC 585, CTA JC 8224, NAC PA-123690; p.82 CTA JC 8150; p.83 CTA, NAC PA-30008; p.84 SHF; p.85 NAC C2082; p.86-87 SA; p.88 NAC PA-74047; p.89 NAC 74084, NAC C14262; p.90 PAM, GA NA C-6-1746; p.91 WS, CTA, GA NA 1068-2; p.92-93 CTA JC 735A; p.94 CTA JC 747B, CTA JC 747A, NAC PA-66815; p.95 CTA JC 8280; p.96 NAC PA-162475; p.97 NAC 80027; p.98 CTA JC 45554; p.99 CTA JC 869A; CTA JC 654, CTA JC 867; p.100 NAC, PAM, GA NA 2736-2; p.101 PAM, PAM, PAM; p.102 NAC PA-648; p.103 OA; p.104 NAC PA-5076; p.105 NAC PA-880, OA, CTA JC 736; p.106 OA, NAC PA-3266, PANL, NAC 172550; p.107 NAC PA-110824, NAC PA-1675, NAC PA-1193, NAC PA-2855; p.108 CTA JC 2456; p.109 CTA JC 245, CTA JC 1771; p.110-111 SA; p.112 NAC; p.113 CTA JC 2543, PAM; p.114 GA NA-3452-2; p.115 NAC; p.116-117 OA.

1920–1929 p.129 WM NA66-1691; p.130 OA/EA, AGO; p.131 OA/EA, p.132 OA/EA; p.133 OA/EA, GA NA-1019-68; p.134 OA/EA; p.135 SHF, NAC PA-127295, TRL; p.136 ANQ; p.137 PAM; p.138 BI 77-57-191; p.139 OA/EA; p.140 Eli-Lilly; p.141 NAC C1350; p.142 TRL, RAWF; p.143 CTA JC 579; p.144 SHF; p.145 GA NA-446-93, GA NA-1644-25; p.146 GA NB-16-417; p.147 PAM/HBC; p.148 PAM/Events 12; p.149 CTA; p.150 TRL, TRL; p.151 NAC C21933, NAC PA-135521; p.152 PAM/N-1936; p.153 NAC C21247; p.154 SHF; p.155-156 CLA P19760211091; p.157 SHF, SHF, SHF; p.158 SHF; p.159 NAC PA-126728; p.160 PAM; p.161 PAA/A-3742; p.162-163 PAA/A-3742.

1930–1939 p.175 CTA JC 116; p.176 CMCP; p.177 VPL 8956-D; p.178-179 CTA JC 995; p.180 NAC PA-51747; p.181 PAM N1819; p.182 HBCA/PAM 363-F-75 N7339, HBCA/PAM 363-F-7 N7340;

p.183 GA NA 1258-119; p.184-185 NAC C31058, CTA JC 4120, NAC, NAC PA-133260, NAC; p.186 NAC PA-145058; p.187 GA, NAC; p.188 NAC, SHF, OA; p.189 OA/EA; p.190-191 CTA (Globe & Mail Collection), NAC PA-124370, NAC; p.192 OA/EA; p.193 NAC PA-133260, OA; p.194-195 USA; p.196-197 NAC C9450, CTA JC 2181, GA NA 2888-7; p.198 NAC PA-136869, NAC C70770; p.199 CTA 8198; p.200 NAC PA-148874; p.201 NAC C74932; p.202 NAC PA-127125; p.203 NAC C74966, NAC PA-117423, NAC C6741; p.204-205 NAC PA-119013; p.206 VPL 1289; p.207 VPL 1276; p.208 CVA 6-68; p.209 NAC PA-76377; p.210-211 NAC PA-107943, ANQ P48 P3713.

1940–1949 p.223 NAC C38723; p.224 PANS; p.225 NAC; p.226 NAC PA-108300; p.227 NAC PA-11363; p.228 NAC PA-112539; p.229 VPL 44965; p.230 OA/EA; p.231 NAC PA-162143; p.232 NAC C27980; p.233 NAC PA-124364; p.234 NAC PA-152119; p.235 SHF; p.236 NAC PA-166565, NAC PA-162143, NAC, NAC; p.237 NAC PA-152838; p.238 NAC PA-152838; p.239 NAC PA-132469; p.240 CBC; p.241 SA, NAC PL-22146, NAC PA-116922; p.242-243 NAC PA-141882; p.244 OA 2398; p.245 NAC/DND PA-128268; p.246 PANS; p.247 NAC C53641; p.248 NAC; p.249 SHF; p.250 Atomic Energy of Canada; p.251 NAC PA-116069; p.252 TRL; p.253 SHF; p.254 NAC PA-130734; p.255 NAC PA-124364; p.256 NAC C6255; p.257 NAC; p.258-259 ANQ.

1950–1959 p.271 CMCP; p.272 TRL; p.273 NAC PA-112083; p.274 PAM; p.275 NAC C79009; p.276 SHF; p.277 NAC C17823, NAC C63976, NBC; p.278 NAC/NFB/Lund: PA-144172; p.279 SA R93-77-46; p.280 NAC PA-151341, NAC PA-151341, NAC; p.281 NAC, NAC PA-124855, YU/TC; p.282 NAC PA-116075; p.283 NAC PA-134581; p.284 NAC PA-142699; p.285 TRL; p.286 OA/EA; p.287 CTA, CTA, CTA, CTA; p.288 HHF; p.289 SHF; p.290 NAC PA-137090; p.291 NAC PA-134184, CMCP EX-82-157, CMCP, NAC PA-114551; p.292-293 CMCP; p.294 YU/TC, NAC PA-111539; p.295 NAC; p.296 NAC PA-151362, NAC, NAC C94168; p.297 NAC, NAC PA-137103; p.298 CP, TRL, NAC PA-111539; p.299 CMCP; p.300 NAC PA-137084; p.301 NAC PA-137074; p.302 CMCP; p.303 NAC PA-1114835, NAC; p.304-305 OA/EA; p.306 NAC PA-163167; p.307 Gabor Szilasi.

1960–1969 p.319 NAC; p.320 SHF, NAC PA-184537; p.321 SHF; p.322-323 CMCP; p.324 NAC PA-137078; p.325 NAC/NFB/Gillat PA-146503, NAC; p.326 CMCP 63-9342C, Ted Grant; p.327 NAC C36222, CP, NAC PA-147472; p.328 CMCP; p.329 CMCP; p.330 NAC, OA/EA, Canadian National Exhibition; p.331 NAC, NAC, NAC; p.332-333 SHF; p.334 NAC PA-137864; p.335 NAC PA-163006; p.336 SHF; p.337 TRL; p.338 CMCP, CMCP, NAC PA-136147; p.339 CMCP, CMCP, CMCP AC 64-3988; p.340 CMCP, CMCP; p.341 CMCP; p.342 CMCP; p.343 NAC, CMCP, CP; p.344 NAC PA-112770, NAC PA-129625, CBC; p.345 CMCP; p.346-347 NAC PA-167031, NAC PA-189363, NAC PA-189360, NAC, NAC; p.348 private collection; p.349 private collection; p.350 CP; p.351 NAC/Gazette PA-117531; p.352 CMCP, CMCP; p.353 NAC PA-139803, NAC PA-111214; p.354 SHF; p.355 CMCP; p.356-357 John Einerson, CP, NAC.

1970–1979 p.369 NAC PA-164027; p.370 NAC PA-129834, NAC PA-129838; p.371 CP, NAC PA-151863; p.372 CP, CP; p.373 Gabor Szilasi; p.374 Richard Pierre; p.375 CP; p.376 NAC PA-1750135; p.377 CP; p.378 CP, CP; p.379 CP; p.380 CMCP; p.381 CP; p.382-383 CMCP; p.384 CMCP; p.385 NAC PA-115039, NAC PA-12986; p.386 NBC, NAC, CMCP, CMCP; p.387 Vancouver Sun; p.388 CMCP, CMCP, CMCP, CMCP; p.389 CMCP, CMCP, CMCP, CMCP; p.390 NAC PA-132340; p.391 CP; p.392 CP; p.393 CP; p.394-395 CP, CP, SHF, SHF; p.396-397 CP, CP; p.398-399 CP; p.400 CP; p.401 CP; p.402 Gabor Szilasi; p.403 Denis Plain, Denis Plain; p.404 Allan Plante; p.405 CP

1980–1989 p.417 CP; p.418 CP; p.419 CP; p.420 CP, CP; p.421 SCTV, ITV; p.422 Keystone; p.423 CP; p.424 Pat Morrow, CP; p.425 CP; p.426 CP, CP; p.427 CP; p.428 CP; p.429 CP; p.430 CP, CP; p.431 CP; p.432 CP; p.433 CP; p.434-435 CP; p.436 Jake Peters; p.437 Kitchener-Waterloo Record; p.438 Vancouver Sun; p.439 Toronto Sun; p.440-441 CP; p.442 CP; p.443 NAC; p.444-445 CP, CP, CP, Cinematheque, reprinted with permission of Crash Post, *Dead Ringers* "The Mantle Clinic II Ltd."; p.446 CP; p.447 CP

1990–1999 p.459 Barbara Woodley/NAC; p.460 CP; p.461 Robert Fréchette, Robert Fréchette; p.462 CP; p.463 CP; p.464 CP; p.465 CP; p.466 Vancouver Sun; p.467 CP; p.468 Adrian Dorst; p.469 Barbara Woodley; p.470 Chris Wahl; p.471 Keystone, Courtesy of Sony Entertainment Canada, Keystone; p.472 Bryce Duffy; p.473 Serge Clément; p.474 CP, CP, CP; p.475 CP, CP; p.476 CP; p.477 CP, CP; p.478 CP; p.479 CP; p.480-481 Bryce Duffy; p.482 CP, p.483 Bryce Duffy; p.484 CP, CP; p.485 CP; p.486 CP; p.487 CP; p.488 Michel St.Jean, *La Voix de l'Est*; p.489 CP, CP; p.490 CP; p.491 CP; p.492 Bryce Duffy; p.493 CP; p.494 CP; p.495 Bryce Duffy; p.496-497 Bryce Duffy.

Literary Sources

Literary Sources Every effort has been made to contact copyright holders. In the event of omission or error, the editor should be notified at Otherwise Inc., 356A Queen Street West, Toronto, Canada M5V 2A2.

1900–1909 Imperial Order Daughters of the Empire, as cited in *Origins of the IODE: A Canadian Women's Movement for God, King and Country 1900–1925* by Doreen Constance Hamilton, University of New Brunswick Thesis; Robert Stanley Weir, as cited in *National Anthems of the World*, Arco Publishing Company Inc.; Henri Bourassa, *Great Britain and Canada: Topics of the Day*, C. O. Beauchemin & Fils; E. Pauline Johnson, *Canadian Born*, Musson Publishing; Wilfrid Laurier, speech at Massey Hall, Toronto, October 14, 1904, printed in *The Globe*, October 15, 1905; Clifford Sifton, as cited in *Clifford Sifton: Volume 2, A Lonely Eminence 1901–1929*, by D.J. Hall, University of British Columbia Press; Anonymous, *The Pioneer Years 1895–1914* by Barry Broadfoot, Doubleday Canada Limited; Ontario Legislative Assembly Committee on Child Labour, as cited in *The Employment of Children and Young Persons in Canada* by the Department of Labour, Canada, F. A. Acland; Lucy Maud Montgomery, *The Annotated Anne of Green Gables*, Oxford University Press; Gilbert Parker, *Northern Lights*, Copp Clark Professional.

1910–1919 Sir Robert Borden, "The Naval Question" *Canada at War*, Macmillan of Canada; George Foster, as cited in *The 1911 General Election: A Study in Canadian Politics*, Copp Clark Professional; "Hindu Invaders Now in the City Harbor on Komagata Maru," *The Vancouver Sun*, Volume 3, Number 711; John McCrae, "In Flanders Fields" as cited in *The New Oxford Book of Canadian Verse in English*, Oxford University Press; Nellie McClung, *In Times Like These*, McLeod & Allen; Louis Hémon, *Maria Chapdelaine*, Macmillan of Canada; Sam Hughes, as cited in *The Hon. Sir Sam Hughes: Canada's War Minister 1911–1916* by Charles F. Winter, Macmillan Company of Canada, Limited; An Act Respecting Military Service, *Statutes of Canada: Acts of the Parliament of the Dominion of Canada*, Joseph de Labroquerie Taché; Ralph Connor, *The Sky Pilot in No Man's Land*, McClelland and Stewart Inc.; Rein-Drive Tractor, *A Saturday Night Scrapbook* edited by Morris Wolfe, New Press.

1920–1929 Lawren Harris, as cited in *There Is No Finality…* by Harry Hunkin, Burns & MacEachern Limited; Robert Edwards, *The Best of Bob Edwards* edited by Hugh A. Dempsey, Hurtig Publishers; W.E. Maclellan, as cited in *The Woman Suffrage Movement in Canada* by Catherine L. Cleverdon, University of Toronto Press; Frederick Banting, as cited in *The Discovery of Insulin* by Michael Bliss, McClelland and Stewart Inc.; Foster Hewitt, *Down the Ice: Hockey Contacts and Reflections*, S. J. Reginald Saunders; Halibut Fishery Treaty, *Treaties and Other International Agreements of the United States of America 1776–1949*, Department of State Publication 8761; James McLachlan, as cited in *The Company Store: James Bryson McLachlan and the Cape Breton Coal Miners 1900–1925* by John Mellor, Doubleday Canada Limited; J.S. Woodsworth, as cited in *Forum: Canadian Life and Letters 1920–1970* edited by J.L. Granatstein and Peter Stevens, University of Toronto Press; Mazo de la Roche, *Jalna*, Pan Books Ltd.; Morley Callaghan, *Strange Fugitive*, McClelland & Stewart Inc.

1930–1939 R.H. Hahn as cited in *The Birth of Radio in Canada: Signing On* by Bill McNeil and Morris Wolfe, Doubleday Canada Limited; Harold Innis, *The Fur Trade in Canada*, University of Toronto Press; Emily Carr, *An Address by Emily Carr*, Stoddart Publishing Co.; Dorothy Livesay, *Right Hand Left Hand*, Press Porcepic Ltd.; William Aberhart, as cited in *Bible Bill: A Biography of William Aberhart* by David R. Elliott and Iris Miller, Reidmore Books; F.R. Scott, *F.R. Scott: Selected Poems*, Oxford University Press; R.B. Bennett, as cited in *The Bennett New Deal: Fraud or Portent?* edited by J.R.H. Wilbur, Copp Clark Professional; Anonymous, as cited in *Ten Lost Years* by Barry Broadfoot, McClelland and Stewart Inc.; Norman Bethune, "Text Books in the Trenches," TRL, Special Collections; William Lyon Mackenzie King, *Canada at Britain's Side*, The Macmillan Company of Canada Limited.

1940–1949 Mark Sorenson, as cited in *None Is Too Many* by Irving Abella and Harold Troper, Lester & Orpen Dennys Limited; Hugh MacLennan, *Barometer Rising*, McClelland and Stewart Inc.; Kotoma Kitagawa, as cited in *Two Monographs on Japanese Canadians*, Arno Press; Northrop Frye, as cited in *Forum: Canadian Life and Letters 1920–1970* edited by J.L. Granatstein and Peter Stevens, University of Toronto Press; Mary Pickford, *Sunshine and Shadow*, Doubleday & Company Inc.; Margaret Brown as cited in *Blackouts to Bright Lights* edited by Barbara Ladouceur & Phyllis Spence, Ronsdale Press; Malcolm Lowry, *Under the Volcano*, Penguin Books; W.O. Mitchell, *Who Has Seen the Wind*, Macmillan of Canada; "The Hero of '48" as cited in *I Chose Canada* by Joseph R. Smallwood, Macmillan of Canada; Paul-Émile Borduas, *Total Refusal* translated by Ray Ellenwood, Exile Editions Ltd.

1950–1959 Pierre Elliott Trudeau, *The Essential Trudeau* edited by Ron Graham, McClelland and Stewart Inc.; Letter to *Saturday Night*, *A Saturday Night Scrapbook* edited by Morris Wolfe, New Press; An Act to Ensure Fair Remuneration to Female Employees, *Statutes of the Province of Ontario*, Baptist Johnston; Farley Mowat,

People of the Deer, McClelland & Stewart Inc.; Vincent Massey, *Speaking of Canada*, The Macmillan Company of Canada Limited; John G. Diefenbaker, as cited in *The Personal Letters of a Public Man* by Thad McIlroy, Doubleday Canada Limited; Gabrielle Roy, *Rue Deschambault*, McClelland & Stewart Inc.; Painters Eleven, as cited in "Painters Eleven 1957" by Park Gallery, Toronto; Lester B. Pearson, *Mike: The Memoirs of the Right Honourable Lester B. Pearson*, University of Toronto Press; Mordecai Richler, *The Apprenticeship of Duddy Kravitz*, McClelland & Stewart; Anonymous, *Remembering the '50s: Growing Up in Western Canada* by Lorraine Blashill, Orca Book Publishers.

1960–1969 Marshall McLuhan, as cited in *Forum: Canadian Life and Letters 1920–1970* edited by J.L. Granatstein and Peter Stevens, University of Toronto Press; Margaret Laurence, *The Stone Angel*, McClelland and Stewart Inc.; Lester Pearson as cited in *Canada's Flag: A Search for a Country* by John Ross Matheson, Mika Publishing Company; Pierre Berton, *The Comfortable Pew*, McClelland & Stewart Inc.; Divorce Act, *Statutes of Canada: Acts of the Parliament of the Dominion of Canada*, Joseph de Labroquerie Taché; George Woodcock, *The Doukhobors*, Oxford University Press; Judy LaMarsh, *Memoirs of a Bird in a Gilded Cage*, McClelland and Stewart Inc.; Gwendolyn MacEwen, *Shadow-Maker*, Macmillan of Canada; Harold Cardinal, *The Unjust Society*, McClelland & Stewart Inc.; Zipp Almasy as cited in *Underground Time* by Ron Verzuh, Deneau Publishers.

1970–1979 René Lévesque, *Memoirs* translated by Philip Stratford, McClelland and Stewart Inc.; David Suzuki, *Genetics and the Future of Man*, University of New Brunswick; Glenn Gould as cited in *Glenn Gould: By Himself and His Friends* edited by John McGreevy, Doubleday Canada Limited; Margaret Atwood, *Survival: A Thematic Guide to Canadian Literature*, House of Anansi Press Limited; Joey Smallwood, *I Chose Canada*, Macmillan of Canada; Dennis Lee, *Wiggle to the Laundromat*, Harper Collins; Henry Morgentaler, as cited in *Morgentaler: The Doctor Who Couldn't Turn Away* by Eleanor Wright Pelrine, Gage Publishing Limited; bp Nichol, *love: a book of remembrances*, Talonbooks; W.P. Kinsella, *Dance Me Outside*, Oberon Press; Leonard Cohen, *Death of a Lady's Man*, McClelland and Stewart Inc.

1980–1989 T.R. Ide, "Canada in the Age of Microelectronics," *Walter L. Gordon Lecture Series*, Volume 4, Canada Studies Foundation; Alice Munro, *The Moons of Jupiter*, Macmillan of Canada; Constitution, *Statutes of the Parliament of the Dominion of Canada*, Joseph de Labroquerie Taché; Ken Dryden, *The Game: A Thoughtful and Provocative Look at a Life in Hockey*, Macmillan of Canada; Jane Jacobs, *Cities and the Wealth of Nations: Principles of Economic Life*, Random House of Canada Limited; Michael Ondaatje, *In the Skin of a Lion*, McClelland and Stewart Inc.; Brian Mulroney, *Canadian Speeches*, August/September 1988; Wayne Gretzky as cited in *The Great One* by Andrew Podnieks, Doubleday Canada; June Callwood, *Jim: A Life with AIDS*, Lester & Orpen Dennys Limited; Stevie Cameron, as cited in *The Montreal Massacre*, Gynergy Books.

1990–1999 Elijah Harper, as cited in *Elijah: No Ordinary Hero* by Pauline Comeau, Douglas & McIntyre; Preston Manning, *Canadian Speeches*, May 1991; Douglas Coupland, *Generation X*, St. Martin's Press; Carol Shields, *The Stone Diaries*, Random House of Canada Limited; Neil Bissoondath, *Selling Illusions: The Cult of Multiculturalism in Canada*, Penguin Books Canada Ltd.; Lucien Bouchard, speech on referendum as translated by *The Globe and Mail*; John Ralston Saul, *The Unconscious Civilization*, House of Anansi Press Limited; Rick Mercer, *Streeters*, Doubleday Canada; Trish Snyder, *Chatelaine*; André Alexis, *Childhood*, McClelland and Stewart Inc.

Index